BUILDING TRUST

BUILDING TRUST
in Business, Politics, Relationships, and Life

Robert C. Solomon
and Fernando Flores

OXFORD
UNIVERSITY PRESS
2001

OXFORD
UNIVERSITY PRESS

Oxford   New York
Athens   Auckland   Bangkok   Bogotá   Buenos Aires   Calcutta
Cape Town   Chennai   Dar es Salaam   Delhi   Florence   Hong Kong   Istanbul
Karachi   Kuala Lumpur   Madrid   Melbourne   Mexico City   Mumbai
Nairobi   Paris   São Paulo   Shanghai   Singapore   Taipei   Tokyo   Toronto   Warsaw

and associated companies in
Berlin   Ibadan

Copyright © 2001 by Robert C. Solomon and Fernando Flores

Library of Congress Cataloguing-in-Publication Data

Solomon, Robert C.

Building trust in business, politics, relationships, and life/Robert C. Solomon
and Fernando Flores.

p. cm.

Includes bibliographical references and index.

ISBN 0-19-512685-8 (alk. paper)

1. Trust. I. Flores, Fernando (Fernando L.), 1954– II. Title.

BF575.T7 S65 2001

158.2—dc21   00-037342

9 8 7 6 5 4 3 2 1

Printed in the United States of America on acid-free paper

For Kathy
For Gloria

For Gustavo Caballero, a friend who understood trust and was a source of trust and compassion

CONTENTS

PREFACE

Trust, like love and freedom, is one of those essential human values that everyone understands—until it comes into question and it is time to put it into practice. Then even the most articulate thinker will tend to descend to clichés ("Trust is important"; "Love is beautiful"; "Live free or die"). Everyone knows trust is important. The question is how we understand trust, and, more important, how we can build trust rather than simply assert its importance.

Building trust begins with an honest understanding of trust, but it also requires everyday routines and practices. Without the practices, that understanding comes to nothing. It is now commonplace for couples and companies to participate in offsite retreats or hire short-term counselors or consultants to transform the relationship or the corporate culture into one of trust. But although such activities can inspire people to recognize and appreciate trust and move them to want to change the way they live and work together, such motivational and teambuilding programs do not, in themselves, produce the desired long-term effects. Enduring results necessitate the embodiment of trust in day-to-day behavior; we need to embrace trust and connect it to our moods and the emotional fabric of our lives. But the key to trust is action, and, in particular, commitment: commitments made and commitments honored.

This book has grown out of many decades of experience consulting with corporations and with couples. In that time, the problem of trust has clearly emerged as *the* problem in human relationships and organizations. We have seen married couples spend small fortunes and a good deal of emotional energy worrying about their joint and individual sexual performance, their ability to communicate, their inability to agree on financial matters, and their unwillingness to share work experiences or leisure activities.

What does not get addressed is the underlying failure, a failure of trust. If two people do not trust each other, it is only too easy to predict that they will not trust each other sexually (a problem many couples mask with the delusion that the dangers of sex provide the real thrill, or by confusing mild sadomasochism with romantic attachment). If two people do not trust each other, it is utterly predictable that they will have trouble communicating, and it is then tempting to blame their problem on one of those ubiquitous but dubious interplanetary models ("men are from Mars, women are from Venus"). The truth is more like this: they fail to make and honor commitments to one another, rendering their emotional lives together uncoordinated and possibly incoherent.

In corporations, the same lack of trust (less the intimacy) betrays itself. Corporate seminars and workshops stress all sorts of skills and motivational attitudes. But what makes most companies falter—leaving aside market forces, bad products, and incompetent management—is the lack of trust. Employees don't trust their supervisors or managers. They may not even trust one another. Managers practice cordial hypocrisy as a matter of course, and consequently, even if they *like* one another, they do not *trust* one another (but often confuse the two). Top executives, at least among themselves, may play a subtler and rougher game. Nevertheless, the companies that function best are almost always those that have trust and harmony at the top, emanating through the organization. Our aim is to help people build trust, establish trust where there has been none, maintain trust when trust is in trouble, and recreate trust even when it seems that trust has been destroyed. To do this, it is necessary first to understand just what trust is and what it is not, and what role it plays in our lives. Again, the answer is to be found in the making and honoring of commitments, especially at the top, which in turn creates a mood of trust throughout an organization.

Between us, we have worked as consultants in corporations for more than forty years. One of us, Fernando Flores, is the president and chief executive officer of Business Design Associates in California, and has effected a thorough and radical restructuring of major corporations in both North and South America and in Europe. The other, Bob Solomon, has designed and delivered programs at several of the largest and most successful global corporations in America and Australia. We are also philosophers and love philosophy. Fernando has a Ph.D. in philosophy and computer science from Berkeley. Bob teaches philosophy and business at the University of Texas at Austin and has been winning teaching awards for thirty years. We both have had a lifelong interest in the dynamics of human relationships.

Fernando has run successful workshops for married couples for almost two decades. Bob regularly does workshops at the Esalen Institute and at other venues that address the topic of love. We met many years ago while Fernando was giving a workshop for couples in New York, although we had known of each other's work for several years. When we met, it was in a conversation in front of a workshop of two hundred people. Other workshops and seminars, and further conversations, followed. Tentative short-term commitments were made. Plans to write a book together about trust not only brought the question of trust into focus; they also made for a crucial interpersonal test.

Writing a book is a challenge in any case, but writing a book on a personal subject, with someone with whom you have never created anything more than a full-day workshop, is the ultimate test. Cowriting is not a diminution of responsibility; it is a special kind of personal commitment that requires a special kind of trust. Competence may be taken for granted, but what cannot be taken for granted are the continuous choices, challenges, breakdowns, frustrations, resolutions, and leaps of faith that constitute authentic trust. But one of the most remarkable aspects of trust is that it seems to disclose what has been present and possible all along—in this case, the very notion of authentic trust that we had been struggling to articulate. It was only at the end of the process, with the manuscript nearly complete, that it became evident that the central thesis of this book was the insight Fernando had brought to the project to begin with: it's not the book itself that counts. It's building the relationship.

We came to the issue of trust by different routes. Fernando's path to the subject was both difficult and traumatic. He was trained as an engineer, but by the age of twenty-nine he was the minister of finance in Salvador Allende's government in Chile. In 1973, when Allende was killed in the coup that brought down his government, Fernando found himself utterly betrayed by the country he loved and had served. He was sent to prison without a trial. He faced execution several times, while his wife and five children waited anxiously.

It is difficult to imagine a more trust-shattering experience. But in the face of prison and possibly imminent execution, Fernando came to realize that the first and most important ingredient in trust is *self*-trust, and the unwavering trust of and in those people closest to you. After three years, Fernando and his family found themselves in exile. They arrived penniless in California, speaking little English. But within a decade, Fernando had earned a Ph.D. in computer science and philosophy and had established himself as a successful entrepreneur. Through the trauma of betrayal, imprisonment, and exile, and with the blessings of self-confidence, a devoted family, and entrepreneurial skills, he came to appreciate, in the most uncompromisingly practical way, the dynamics of trust and distrust. Today, in his work as a global consultant, he finds that trust and distrust have become the major concern of successful businesses (whether they know it or not), whether these businesses are large corporations or small, entrepreneurial enterprises. Creating trust has become the primary goal of his business practices.

Bob has had considerably less trauma in his life. He experienced no such dramatic betrayals, no such need for the leaps of faith that trust sometimes requires. For him, as for most people, trust was the invisible medium that he simply assumed in his personal and most of his professional relationships. He came to appreciate trust not by way of betrayal but in terms of his lifelong fascination with human emotions and the complexities of intimate relationships.

Disputing the usual view of emotions as disruptions of and intrusions into rational life, Bob has long argued that it is our emotional stance, not our abstract beliefs or our abilities to calculate, reason, and theorize, that makes us human and defines much of our world. He has been particularly intrigued by romantic love in all its manifestations, and, with it, the practical dynamics of relationships. Thinking about love has naturally led to thinking about intimacy, fidelity, jealousy, and trust. Meanwhile, he has written and consulted with corporate executives on questions of integrity and trust, and has come to see that the questions he asks about personal relationships and the situations he confronts in business settings are connected. Like Fernando, he has come to appreciate that love, business life, and politics are not three separate realms but practical dimensions of a single social world in which human relationships are primary. And what binds the best and most powerful relationships together is what we will call *authentic trust*.

We are indebted to a great many people, including the German philosopher Martin Heidegger and a number of contemporary analysts, for our ideas here. But we have written about trust, not what other people have thought about trust, so we have kept references and pointed disagreements to a minimum. We are also indebted to a large number of people who have attended our workshops and seminars, and to the companies that have trusted us to delve into their innermost workings. For reasons of confidentiality and in order to avoid any misunderstandings, we have decided as a matter of principle to mention no companies (or real-life couples) by name in this book. Examples are based on but not identifiable as genuine cases (and we have drawn them from several dozen different companies, many of which have similar problems). Finally, we wish to give special thanks for help and encouragement to Betty Sue Flowers, Hubert Dreyfus, Charles Spinosa, Kelly Curry, Joanne Ciulla, and Kathleen Higgins.

BUILDING TRUST

INTRODUCTION

The great philosopher Saint Augustine, when asked to define what time was, found himself puzzled. Until he was asked, he knew perfectly well what time was. But once asked, he had no idea what to say. And that was in those supposedly relaxed days in northern Africa when the problem was not—as in today's nanosecond world—*making* time. Time was there (like it or not) for the taking.

The problem with trust is both similar and different. Asked to define what trust is, we find ourselves puzzled. Before we were asked, we knew what trust was, but now we find ourselves groping for answers—"It's a feeling, I can't describe it"; "it's knowing (or predicting) that the other person will come through for you." But more important, we don't know how to create trust, or how to build trust in circumstances of distrust, on the ruins of a trust already betrayed. Couples and people in organizations spend retreats together, enjoying one another's company, airing their misgivings about how they function together in the real world, making all sorts of resolutions to understand and trust one another in the future. But then back to work and everyday life they go, and old patterns snap into place.

To understand trust is to be able to build trust into our everyday practices and relationships, and to develop institutions in which such practices and relationships are not only possible but mandatory. There is nothing exotic about this. We are not talking about creating trust between Serbs and Kosovars in the midst of ethnic warfare. We are simply talking about ordinary trust, at home and at the office, where conversations, not weapons, are the only tools we need. But they must be the right kinds of conversations, not cordial hypocrisy and not the sort of cynicism and resignation in which everyone laments but nothing can be done.

The problem of trust may be, first of all, a question of understanding, but such understanding is meaningful only in the pursuit of a practice, a day-to-day routine, a way of being—or, for organizations or nations, the development of institutions of trust. Most people in relationships, whether friendships, marriages, working partnerships, or casual love affairs, after some sort of courtship period, find themselves comfortably submerged in trust, taking each other for granted (at least within certain limits), not even thinking about the dreadful things they could easily do to each other.

Asked whether they trust each other, two spouses or lovers will readily say "Yes." Asked what this means, they will probably respond something like this: "Well of course I trust Sally. I *love* her!" Or, "Yes, I never even have to think about it." Or simply, "Of course. We've been together for more than ten years." It is when trust is violated or betrayed that these simple answers no longer suffice. When the difficult task of rebuilding trust begins, many people throw in the towel, giving up on what may have been a life-defining relationship by projecting future difficulties. "I can't live or work with him anymore, because I no longer trust him." In other words, when trust is most at issue, we all too easily tend to give up on it. The situation is much the same in organizations and political institutions. These days, people are more than eager to agree that trust is essential to a smoothly working, efficient corporate culture. They are similarly eager to confirm the trust that extends throughout their organizations. But if asked to define exactly what this trust consists in, they treat us to clichés and misunderstandings. Short of open warfare, the worst of these is what we call *cordial hypocrisy:* the strong tendency of people in organizations, because of loyalty or fear, to pretend that there is trust when there is none, being polite in the name of harmony when cynicism and distrust are active poisons, eating away at the very existence of the organization.

In such circumstances, instead of being forums for addressing problems and facing criticism, discussions and meetings are painful in their strained propriety and frustrating because they fail to provide the opportunity to build trust and solve problems by way of the kind of discussion that releases people's creative juices and amplifies their sense of solidarity at the same time. Instead, people sit on their ideas (if they have any, in the tumult of resentment and frustration they feel), abstain from criticism (especially of the boss), and courteously agree with plans they know cannot possibly work. After the meetings, outside the channels where objections might be effective, sarcastic criticism will be as free-flowing as gossip, ad hominem attacks, and cynicism. But the same employees, managers, and executives who insist on trust in the organization turn out to be those who have given up on trust, and worse, make building trust all the more difficult.

Top executives can usually expect both overt respect and obedience from their employees and managers. After all, the executives have the power to fire them. But whether or not the leaders earn their trust is a different issue, and executives ignore the difference at their peril. Without trust, the corporate community is reduced to a group of resentful wage slaves and defensive, if not ambitious, managers. People will do their jobs, but they will not offer their ideas, or their enthusiasm, or their souls. Without trust the corporation becomes not a community but a brutish state of nature, a war of all against all in which employment tends to be nasty, brutish, and short. And yet top executives can almost routinely be expected to say, "Yes, people in this company trust one another." It is, after all, much easier to say this than to recognize and fix the problem.

Trust is not always a good thing. Trust can be foolish, naïve, gullible, and blind. And trust ought never to be taken for granted. That is why we insist that the issue is *building trust—* that is, creating trust, maintaining trust, restoring trust once it has been lost or betrayed. We want to suggest that this requires a radical revision of our conception of trust. Our thesis, to put it simply, is that trusting is something that we individually *do;* it is something we make, we create, we build, we maintain, we sustain with our promises, our commitments, our emotions, and our sense of our own integrity. Trust is not, contrary to what recent authors have written, a medium, an atmosphere, a "lubricant," social "glue," a lucky break for one society or another, or some mysterious social "stuff."[1] Trust is an option, a choice. It is an active part of our lives, not something that has to be there from the beginning, or that can be taken for granted. It involves skills and commitment, not just good luck or mutual understanding.

The focus of trust—or what we will call *authentic trust*—is not just the hoped-for outcome of this or that event or transaction. Trust is not merely reliability, predictability, or what is sometimes understood as *trustworthiness*. It is always the *relationship* within which trust is based and which trust itself helps create. Authentic trust does not necessitate the exclusion of distrust. To the contrary, it embraces the possibilities of distrust and betrayal as an essential part of trust. To be somewhat grim in our initial characterization of trust, *it entails the possibility of betrayal.* The loss of trust is not mere disappointment. That is why trust is often evident only in the event of a breakdown. Like love, trust often becomes most palpable in the breach. ("You don't miss your water till the well runs dry.") Building trust means coming to terms with the possibility of breach and betrayal.

The comparison with love is illuminating in a number of ways. Like love, trust at first may seem both miraculous and perfectly natural. It "happens" to us, or we "fall into" it. Eventually, we get used to it; we take it for granted. But it then suffers from lack of attention, and sometimes explodes in a vehement trauma of misunderstanding, disappointment, even betrayal. Trust, like love, may seem to fail us, but truly, *we* fail at trust or love. But then we get more sophisticated. We learn that trust, like love, is an emotional skill. It requires judgment. It requires vigilant attention. It requires conscientious action. It involves all of the intricate reciprocities of a human relationship (even in cases in which it remains "unrequited"). Marriage, whatever else it may be (a contract, an institution, a license for sex, the culmination of romance, the start of a family, an economic arrangement, the fabric of society), requires vigilance about trust of the most profound kind.[2]

Moreover, like love, trust is one of those odd things in life that we feel we know so well—until we try to describe it.

Indeed, it is something that we all think we know how to do "naturally." But trusting, like loving, must be taught—and learned. It can be "instituted" (as love has been, through the modern institutions of romance and marriage, over the past several centuries in the West).[3] We distinguish between naïve (or "puppy") love and the mature love that has acquired wisdom as well as passion. So, too, we will distinguish what we call authentic trust from mere "simple" trust, and from blind trust, with which it is often confused. It is by way of authentic trust, as in "true love," that one builds and creates relationships and new possibilities—even "new worlds"—despite the obstacles and the suspicion of distrust, even the trauma of betrayal, through caring and commitment.

Trust, like love, is an emotional skill, an ongoing, dynamic aspect of relationships. We don't just fall in love. We decide to love. We decide to pursue love, to persevere in love. So, too, we do not simply find ourselves trusting, after months or perhaps years of comfortable familiarity. We make decisions to trust. We make promises and tacit commitments. We see them through. We come to have expectations of others, and we respond to the fulfillment or frustration of those expectations. Trust isn't something we "have," or a medium or an atmosphere within which we operate. Trust is something we do, something we make. Our mutual choices of trust determine nothing less than the kinds of beings we are and the kinds of lives we will live together.

Trust might also be compared to freedom as one of the basic human goods. Indeed, we want to say that trust is a kind of freedom, not only the freedom from suspicion and distrust but the freedom to realize all sorts of possibilities, especially with other people. We conceive of trust as a "clearing" in our lives in which all sorts of cooperative and otherwise risky activities are possible. President Nixon's notorious "enemies list" structured his ill-fated incumbency. He forbade members of his administration to talk to reporters or politicians on the list, and he consequently so narrowed the range of his administration's power to practice politics that the presidency became dysfunctional long before the actual unfolding of the Watergate scandal. Whatever else President Ford may have done in bringing to an end "our long national nightmare" in pardoning Nixon, it was clear that not only did he free up the three branches of government, which had been bogged down for months, but he exuded a spirit of openness that was a relief to every American and millions of non-American diplomats, businesspeople, and politicians, whatever their politics.

Anyone who has experienced the emotional turmoil and frustrations of "office politics" knows full well how distrust limits one's ability to act, to speak, even to breathe easily and engage in one's work. The resolution of mutual suspicion and distrust, or liberation from office politics (for example, by going to work "for oneself," an option taken yearly by millions of fed-up American workers), is freedom, perhaps one of the most important nonpolitical freedoms that one can enjoy. (Political freedoms, it should be noted, also involve a certain degree of trust. Freedom of speech is an empty option when it doesn't include the possibility of being listened to and taken seriously, or if it is constantly threatened by lawsuits, personal violence, and other repercussions and retributions. So, too, can freedom of religion be an invitation to sectarian warfare if it is not coupled with tolerance and trust.)

The freedom provided by trust is the freedom to engage in projects that one could not or would not undertake on one's own. The freedom provided by trust is the freedom to approach and engage with strangers whom one may in fact never lay eyes on, as in the booming e-commerce economy. The freedom provided by trust is the freedom to think for oneself and speak up with one's ideas. It includes as its consequence (not its cost) the freedom to be questioned and criticized—and the right to be recognized and (if deserving) rewarded.

This is what office politics makes impossible. When contributions are rewarded for political reasons instead of on merit, the very notion of "having a good idea" goes by the wayside. When a trusting approach to strangers is repaid by being "ripped off," not only is the idea of doing business with those whom you do not know dealt a blow; the very freedom of the marketplace is compromised. When you can't trust your colleagues to cooperate on a project (for example, because they will steal your ideas or take the credit themselves), the basic freedom of doing business—*entrepreneurship*—is damaged.

"Office politics" refers to a kind of petty warfare, with enemies and back-stabbing and hidden sabotage—in short, with a breakdown in trust. Nothing is so compelling as warfare, and if a war is happening in the cubicles, the neighborhood fight looms much larger than the more distant struggle for quality and market share in which the company as a whole is engaged. Everyone complains and then agrees, "Let's get rid of politics around here." But the effective practice of politics, even office politics, is absolutely necessary in the absence of a dictator. Many businesses that have turned away from the old command-and-control model end up reverting to that model because employees and managers don't know how to practice politics in a culture of trust.

Trust is something that must be *learned*. The absence of warfare isn't yet peace, but instead of warfare there can be dialogue and honest, mutual struggle on the road to shared commitments, which are the foundation of trust. The building of trust is political. In the absence of a culture of trust, on the other hand, politics turns into war, where there are a few winners and a lot of losers. A company dominated by office politics is a company with a lot of losers.

The German sociologist Niklas Luhmann stresses that trust is a way of dealing with complexity in an increasingly complex society.[4] There is a deep truth to this. The paradigm of trust is not found in the simplicity of a familiar relationship. Rather, it exists in the new complexity of the world and the global economy. Trust not only lets us increase complexity in our lives (and thus simplify them at the same time); it also changes our lives in dramatic ways, allowing us to explore in new directions, to experiment and express ourselves in our relationships in ways that would otherwise be unthinkable. And it allows us to grow and change and mellow and deepen in all the ways that merely provincial trust and distrust distort and prohibit.

In a relationship, whether a friendship, a romantic affair, or a long-standing marriage, trust is also a form of freedom. If a woman doesn't trust her husband, for instance, in the realm of managing money, it becomes necessary for her to expend an enormous amount of time overseeing, counseling, questioning, challenging, and arguing with his dubious decisions about investments and purchases, whether major or minor. Only someone who has never had (or imagined) such an experience could fail to see the situation as a trap, a sinkhole of time and energy, and a cause of frustration and fury that will inevitably spill over into the rest of the relationship. A husband who becomes jealous of his wife's flirtatious personality (which is most likely one of the reasons he married her) soon finds himself playing the compulsive private detective–prosecutorial role, cross-examining her about her every movement, thinking nothing but jealous thoughts whenever she is away, overinterpreting every comment and gesture. The restrictions this behavior imposes on one's life are clear, as is the tremendous sense of freedom (which emerges in pure form in situation comedies on television) that accompanies the full resolution of such suspicions.

It is one of the prominent myths of our society that freedom belongs essentially to the individual, and a free society is one that leaves the individual be. But in addition to the usual objections about the importance of community and the emptiness of a freedom without the necessary conditions and services that depend on other people (health care, education, a clean environment, safe streets, an invigorating as opposed to a degrading culture), one must note that such rabid individualism ignores the extent to which even the most individualistic of heroes— for example, the entrepreneur—depends on a network of people to bring his or her ideas to fruition, to purchase his or her products or services, to maintain his or her reputation so that the new company can grow and prosper. What's more, the celebration of American heroes too often ignores what each of them will quickly disclose in interviews—"I owe it all to my beloved spouse, mother, father, children, mentor."

We are not born into this world alone, and most of us are rarely alone in any significant way. Life is made up of friendships, partnerships, marriages, associations, organizations, institutions, and acquaintances. Any conception of the good life (except to the rare hermit or lone mountaineer) that leaves out the importance of human relationships is pathetic and unrealistic. And all of these relationships require trust.[5] Philosophers have long tried to delimit the good life by appeals to general (even "absolute") principles, but even when relationships are subject to rational or religious principles, they are certainly not defined by them, nor are our decisions—whether or not to trust a friend with our life savings; whether or not to get married—made by appealing to transpersonal principles.[6] We decide whether or not to trust, and when we do—or when we do not—the consequences are dramatic. This is what makes it necessary to begin by trusting trust, because without it, all proclamations of goodness fall into self-righteousness, alienation, and loneliness.

Trust forms the foundation, or the dynamic precondition, for any free enterprise system. What constitutes that freedom is not only the right to make promises (to buy, to produce, to sell, to hire and pay, to give one's labor or one's expertise), but, just as important, the responsibility for keeping promises, following through on one's offers, making good on one's commitments. The individual entrepreneur, like the giant corporation, depends on trust—including self-trust—to function in the business world. Francis Fukuyama has argued that trust is the precondition for prosperity, and that we are in danger of frittering it away.[7] High-trust societies, he shows, are outstanding in their potential for forming wide-reaching and successful cooperative partnerships. Low-trust societies, by contrast, often tend to be economic disaster areas and can certainly be terrible places to live.

Trust also provides the preconditions of civil society, civil not just in the sense of "getting along" but in the much stronger, ancient sense of a *polity,* an organized and coordinated community. (Corporations, for example, are best conceived of not as legal fictions but as coordinated communities.)[8] But trust in politics is a matter of some curiosity in its own right. History is full of peoples who trusted the most horrible monsters (Hitler, obviously; Mussolini, until he overstepped his demand that the trains run on time; Slobodan Milosevic, until he lost one war too many). But America has a long history and ideology of *distrust* of government ("Big Government"). Nevertheless, Americans traditionally display a good deal of trust. Complaints about even minor inefficiencies in local government are a reflection of the extent to which Americans take the legitimacy of their operations for granted. Delayed postal service, for example, is a common matter for grievance, but this simply indicates that people ordinarily do trust postal workers to deliver their mail on time, with little or no monitoring or attention.

The ideology of mistrust in government, now so much a part of the American myth, is foolishly misconceived. James Fallows of *U.S. News and World Report* wrote recently, "There are moments in history on which we look back and say, 'What were those people thinking?' ... A generation from now, people will look back on us and wonder what we were thinking on one fundamental issue, the role and purpose of government. Democrats have done very little to challenge the modern Republican proposition that government is simply evil, that it is wasteful, oppressive, misguided and inefficient." But what people say about trust is not always (or even usually) a good indication of their trust. And we might add, just for good measure, that a lack of trust in government can be as dangerous as a blind trust in government. Indeed, without trust, there can be no government, no polity at all.

For all of us, in our personal and professional lives, in our roles as citizens and consumers, in our roles as leaders and as members of the world community, "we have to learn to trust one another." So Václav Havel pleaded to his people in an impassioned speech after the Velvet Revolution that brought an end to fifty years of Communism and terror in Czechoslovakia. So, too, we plead to each other, in a world that is in some ways just beginning. This book is a plea for building trust, in aspects of our lives where trust is just beginning, or unknown, or even where trust has been betrayed, trampled, and seemingly destroyed.

All of this is promissory and broadly philosophical, but the reader should know exactly what we offer in the pages to follow. We intend this book to be thoroughly practical, but this does not mean that we provide a "recipe" or "ten-step plan" for building trust in a corporation, a marriage, or a society. What we do try to provide is a vision and an understanding of trust that makes building trust both possible and practical. Talk about trust too easily tends to invite banalities—for instance, "Trust is important." This tendency is aggravated by the temptation to dress up the banalities in professional jargon. So let us begin by summarizing, in fairly blunt terms, the somewhat against-the-grain vision of trust that we promote in this book:

- Trust, compared to love and freedom, will help us avoid the negativity implied by the widespread (if often unrecognized) view that trust is essentially risk and dependency. Trust is an opening up of the world, not a diminution of it.
- Although trust often seems invisible ("transparent," simply taken for granted), it is the result of continuous attentiveness and activity. Trust, once established, easily recedes into the background, into a familiar and therefore barely conscious set of habits and practices. But trust should not be confused with its background status. Trust often becomes visible (in retrospect) only when it has been challenged or violated.
- Trust is not a "medium," or the "glue" that holds relationships and societies together. It is not a "lubricant" for social relations. It is not an "atmosphere." It is not "stuff."
- Trust is dynamic. It is part of the vitality, not the inert foundation, of relationships. It involves personal responsibility, commitment, and change.
- Trust is a social practice, not a set of beliefs. It is a "how to," not a "knowing that." It is an aspect of culture and the product of cultivation, not just a matter of individual psychology or attitude.
- Trust should not be confused with the poisonous practice that we call cordial hypocrisy, the defensive pretense of trust and agreement that hides fear and resentment and makes honest communication impossible.
- The problem of trust is not merely an analytic or theoretical

one. The problem is practical: how to create and maintain trust; how to move from distrust to trust, from a breach of trust to recovery. We thus distinguish simple trust from what we call authentic trust.

- Thinking and talking about trust will not only influence our beliefs but also change our behavior in the world and with one another.

- How we think about trust (whether we confuse it, for example, with total control, with blind or simple trust, or with reliance, risk, and probability) makes trust possible, difficult, or even impossible. Trust (like love and freedom) involves any number of self-promoting and self-defeating prophecies.

- Breaches of trust do not mark the end of trust but are part of the process of trusting. (There are many kinds of breaches, from mistakes to betrayal and treachery. It is important not to confuse them or to assume that all breaches are betrayals.)

- Trust(ing), not trustworthiness, is the issue. The existential question is *how* to trust, not just who can be trusted. (Trust is not only earned; it must be *given*.)

- Trust is a matter of reciprocal *relationships*, not of prediction, risk, and reliance.

- Trust is transformative. It is not a matter of trusting or being trusted so much as it is a matter of changing each other and the relationship through trust. This is what we mean when we talk about "dynamic relationships."

- Trust is a matter of making and keeping commitments, and the problem of trust is not loss of confidence but the failure to cultivate commitment making.

- Commitments do not limit freedom but are its precondition and expression.

- Trust is a matter of mood and emotional skills, a function of the imagination as well as the product of negotiation and understanding.

- Our moods and emotions are engagements in the world. They are skillful practices, not mere "feelings." They do not just happen to us. We are not merely victims.

- Our moods and emotions change with our practices. Trust is historical, but it is not so much tied to the past as it is pregnant with the future.
- Our emotional practices can change and be cultivated. We can (and must) learn to trust.
- When Francis Fukuyama famously distinguishes between "high-trust" and "low-trust" societies, he is ultimately referring to emotional practices that can change and be cultivated. Thus high-trust and low-trust societies are not fixed destinies or historical necessities.
- Trust involves sincerity, authenticity, integrity, virtue, and honor (matters of *ethics*). It is not a "neutral" character trait, not just a cultural pattern, not just a matter of individual "good judgment." It is not a matter of unthinking habit (simple trust) but a matter of conscientious integrity, *authentic* trust.
- The worst enemies of trust are cynicism, selfishness, and a naïve conception of life in which one expects more than one is willing to give. Resentment, distrust, and inauthenticity are the result.
- Self-trust is the most basic and most often neglected form of trust. Distrust is often a projection of missing self-trust.
- Trust goes hand in hand with truth. Lying is always a breach of trust.
- What is wrong with lying, in turn, is that it breaches trust. Whether or not telling the truth is a duty, a "categorical imperative," whether or not it serves the best interests of the greatest number of people, whether or not it reflects well on the virtue or character of the individual, telling the truth establishes trust and lying destroys it.
- Authentic trust can never be taken for granted, but must be continuously cultivated through commitments and truthfulness.
- True leadership, whatever else it may be, can be based on nothing less.

I

TRUSTING
TRUST

To what extent can we trust one another? The world is shrinking; our individual worlds are growing. Can the minorities and the little nations trust the ruling majorities and the giant economic powers, and vice versa? Can the poor and the workers of the world trust those who determine their lives and their livelihoods? Can we trust the Eastern Europeans to get their houses in order? Can we trust ourselves to do the same? Can we trust our leaders to serve the interests of the people in times of increasing uncertainty? Can we trust the market—or, rather, the leaders of our largest corporations—to act in the public interest? Or is everything now a contractual deal to benefit only those who invest and consume? Can we trust our neighbors, whether down the block, across the city or the country, or halfway around the globe? Can we trust the people we work with, and work for, or do we expend our energies instead on protecting ourselves and minimizing our vulnerability? We hope that we can trust in these ways, but it should not be taken for granted.

It is often suggested that widespread distrust is stimulating the current interest in trust. We think that the truth is more subtle and interesting: there is more trust in the world than ever before, and the increasingly global dependence on trust spurs both our interest in and our need for trust. In situations of distrust, people do not talk about trust but rather develop strategies for coping with its absence. This was certainly the reality in the old Soviet bloc. No one was talking about the need for trust then, in a situation where distrust had assumed nightmare proportions.[9] By contrast, Americans demonstrate an exceptionally high level of trust in their government on a practical and day-to-day level, and readily react to even a hint of betrayal. What people *say* about trust often differs from what their behavior suggests.

We generally trust the products we buy; we thoughtlessly stake our lives on them (cars, pharmaceuticals, packaged foods, airplanes, parachutes, bungee cords). We trust the people who serve us, often without checking their credentials. (Do most of us ever look at our doctors' or dentists' professional degrees? How do you know that the waitress did not spit in your soup or drop your sandwich on the way from the kitchen? How many people double-check the pills dispensed by their pharmacists? How do we know in an emergency that we haven't hired the Three Stooges as our electricians and plumbers—that is, unless the calamitous results are obvious?) Despite the notorious scams and phonies, our attitude toward most of our business transactions is one of trust, mixed with a certain amount of prudence. If one really accepted the warning "caveat emptor" (let the buyer beware), it would be difficult to be a consumer at all.

Trust on Trial

Trust. The rock group Metallica assures us in a popular song that "Nothing Else Matters." This sentiment was the 1990s version of the Beatles' epochal but atavistic pronouncement in the 1960s that "All You Need Is Love." (The Beatles were wrong, as the nascent feminist movement quickly made clear.)[10] Love is lovely, but respect, autonomy, fair salaries, and full citizenship are also necessary.

So too with trust. Trust is an essential aspect of relationships, business, and politics, but it is not the single answer to all our ills.[11] In retrospect, given the post–cold war KGB revelations of recent years, the strategic wisdom that "you can't trust the Soviets" proved to be justified. Distrust, not trust, was the course to follow. Even in domestic politics, there is always room for healthy skepticism. In business, trust must be carefully cultivated and cautiously evaluated, and a merely "trusting" businessperson would not long be in business at all. Even where there is trust, contracts are appropriate and often necessary, if not for enforcement, then to specify commitments and expectations. In marriages, husbands and wives may pretend to trust each other precisely when they do not, because the alternatives—suspicion, uncertainty, confrontation, divorce—are too painful to contemplate. But the price of such merely pretended trust—cordial hypocrisy—is a kind of poison that corrodes relationships even as it seems to hold them together. Much the same can be said about cordial hypocrisy in an organization, where feigned politeness and "team spirit" may mask resentments and inefficiencies that are destroying the company.

How much do we trust one another? Upper-income couples now routinely sign "prenuptial agreements," in the flush of love already anticipating an eventual breakup and divorce. Divorce now claims nearly two-thirds of our marriages, suggesting that our sense of commitment and consequently our warrant for trust is not what it used to be, even in the most intimate relationships. A virtual explosion of liability suits similarly suggests that the "normal" (that is, extralegal) bonds of trust have broken down. Without getting into the thicket of arguments about the harms and benefits of our current tort system, we can say with some confidence that the dramatic increase in courtroom complaints reflects considerable misunderstanding among our fellow citizens and institutions regarding the ordinary expectations of everyday life. In corporations, the epidemic of downsizing and restructuring has taken its toll. Loyalty is often said to be an inappropriate or foolish virtue, and distrust and defensiveness rather than shared purpose have all but destroyed the morale of many major companies.

Indeed, a walk down the street in a strange city—or even in our own hometowns—has become a trial for trust. Home burglary alarm systems, antitheft devices in our cars, ever-improving security systems for computers and the even faster-increasing demand for them all point to a widespread distrust of our fellow citizens. In the past two decades, our loss of trust in doctors, lawyers, economists, and other professionals and experts has been dramatic and, for conscientious practitioners in those professions, traumatic. Loss of trust in public officials—for example, those in the American Congress, the presidency, the Supreme Court, and similar institutions in nations around the world—has resulted in widespread cynicism and some acts of horrific violence (the bombing of embassies and of the Federal Building in Oklahoma City being some of the more extreme examples).

These different realms of trust and distrust require considerably different modes of understanding. In a sense, trust is not one thing but many. Trust exists wholly in its particulars, in each and every instance of the practice of trust. There is no Platonic form or ideal of trust, no single paradigm case, although one can make generalizations about trust. One of these observations is that the nature of trust has been called into question in part because of an apparent epidemic of distrust. But the other side of this observation is that trust has never been more relevant or important; it has come into question precisely because, in a free society and a growing free-market economy, it is trust and not power or fear that is essential to our well-being and the possibility of a "new world order." That new world order, if it is to be more than simply the disruption of old power hierarchies, will be defined by the trust it builds among nations, among consumers and the com-

panies that serve them, and among increasingly powerful corporations and the citizens of the world.

In much of the current literature, the word "trust" has
became a trigger for nostalgia, a reminder of supposedly
more simple times when Americans did not lock their doors,
when they routinely picked up hitchhikers and talked to
strangers. There was a time when people paid more attention
to their manners than to the safety of their wallets or to fears
about their physical well-being. It was a world before
prenuptial agreements, liability suits, incessant calls for
impeachment proceedings, and concealed-handgun laws. It
was a world in which marriage was considered a lifelong
commitment, when "a man's word was his bond," when business was conducted on a handshake, and a promise made by a
politician was taken seriously as a promise, however doubtful
the voters might have been about whether that promise
would be kept. Today, a politician's promise is worth less than
the day-old newspaper that prints it. Business is conducted
only with lawyers or a legal team in tow, with the threat of
litigation always palpably present. Divorce has become a matter of right and even of convenience, a state of affairs that
many commentators have correctly identified with the flag-
ging significance of commitment—and hence trust—in our
society.[12]

To be sure, one can find serious fault with the old-fash-
ioned ways of doing and thinking about things. Many of
those lifelong marriages were pure hell, and both the spouses
and the children might have been better off after a divorce.
But is it the case that trust is diminishing in the world, as we
are so often told? Or could it be that it is merely being relo-
cated to new institutions, to new kinds of leaders and entrepreneurs? We have tended to think of trust as something
established, something simply to be taken for granted, at least
among friends, family, and neighbors. But in the fast-changing world of the twenty-first century, trust must be recon-
ceived in terms of rapid change, converging societies in a
global market, and a world that is (perhaps for the first time)
self-consciously making its own history.

Alternatives to Trust: Fear, Control, Power

Business executives these days talk a great deal about trust, but mainly to bemoan its absence in their own companies. Downsizing is taking its toll. Company loyalty is a thing of the past, and sabotage on the job has reached crisis proportions. Everyone agrees that more trust is needed and that distrust is costly and inefficient, not to mention unpleasant and sometimes humiliating. But when it comes to building trust, creating more trust, combating distrust with trust, the arguments seem to hit a dead end. One of our colleagues, who also consults for major corporations, reported that following a lecture to several hundred executives of one of America's largest corporations on the importance of trusting employees, the first question he got was "But how do we control them?" It is a telling question, one that indicates that the questioner (and perhaps most of the executives in the room) did not understand either the thesis of the lecture or the nature of trust. And that, perhaps, is the hardest point to get across—that trust and control must not be confused. Increasing trust within a company does not increase control. Rather, by easing the reins of control, it improves efficiency, effectiveness, cooperation, team spirit, employee morale, and chances for success in an increasingly competitive world.

Niccolò Machiavelli gives us some famous advice in *The Prince*. Asking, rhetorically, "Whether 'tis better [for a leader] to be loved or feared," he answers unequivocally: better to be feared, because it is "safer." His reasoning is not flattering: "For it may be said of men in general that they are ungrateful and fickle, dissemblers, evaders of danger, and greedy of gain. So long as you shower benefits upon them, they are yours ... [but] men have less hesitation in offending one who makes himself beloved than one who makes himself feared. For love holds by a bond of obligation which, as mankind is bad, is broken on every occasion whenever it is in the interest of the obliged party to break it."[13]

In other words, people cannot be trusted; they must be controlled or threatened. Leaders cannot trust their people except insofar as they can be controlled through fear. The view is happily dead, in most quarters, that marriage and family are held together by fear of the patriarch, but vestiges of that view still exist, evidenced by rampant child and spousal abuse and the fear evoked in men by women with full independence and autonomy. In the corporation, rule by fear has become "the law of the jungle," however kind and humane company policy may be. (Metaphors of war and brutality have contributed much more than a literary flair to the epidemic of distrust in our major corporations.)[14] Twenty-year veterans have no more job security than their newly hired colleagues, and all too often downsizing gives little heed to hard work or merit. It is not surprising that Machiavelli's name keeps surfacing in management literature, along with Attila the Hun, Genghis Khan, and other Masters of the Universe.[15]

The suggestion that people can't be trusted would have shocked the community-minded Christians of the early sixteenth century, who had been raised on a philosophy of love, and who had recently renewed their acquaintance with Aristotle, who was concerned with virtue. Aristotle had held that the very basis of a decent political community had to be virtuous people who could trust one another in politics and commerce as in battle. Even the Renaissance in Europe depended on newfound trust—trust in humanity, trust in the humanities, trust in the ancients, trust in each other, and continuing trust in God. One could trace, perhaps with a sense of nostalgia, the transformation of political theory from Aristotle's trust-laden concept of the statesman as inherently noble and civic-minded to the Machiavellian notion of politicians as essentially self-serving and corrupt, a politics of suspicion instead of politics as a continuation of personal virtue and ethics.

Similarly cynical thoughts have punctuated the whole of human history, back to the Greeks and the Romans and some Confucians (for example, Xunzi) in ancient China. The underlying supposition is that there is a fixed human nature and that its essence is selfishness. Prudent strategy therefore dictates generalized distrust. Trust, conversely, is foolishness. In such a world, trust has no sensible place. The only way to proceed is with power. Talking about trust, even mentioning the subject, can only be viewed as an act of manipulation and deception. When corporate consultants and executives speak of "empowerment"—an apparent offer to negotiate sharing power in return for trust—employees quite prudently respond with suspicion. Empowerment too often means responsibility and blame without any real authority or autonomy. And where the overriding culture of the company is one of command and control, the result is massive distrust and cynicism.

Trust and control are incompatible because the core of trust involves freedom. To trust people is to count on their sense of responsibility (or perhaps their sense of integrity), believing that they will choose to act in a trustworthy manner, while recognizing the possibility that they may choose to betray the trust. To trust someone is to expect that he or she will understand our expectations and figure out a way to overcome obstacles. But because of its essential link to freedom, trust always involves a risk. It is always fragile. And so those in power often prefer to command by using that power, and not by employing trust. The new language of business requires that this be disguised, so the imposition of power is often presented as a matter of trust. But to expect one's employees to act as directed under the threat of punishment is not to trust them, any more than a man who imprisons his wife in the house can be said to trust her. But, it may be argued, why should one accept the risks and uncertainties of trust rather than the security of power? In other words, why trust? Why not power?

Power can be understood in two different (though often interconnected) ways: first as sheer force, as a threat, through the imposition of fear; and second as authority, *legitimate* power, power that has been earned (as when one becomes "an authority on Shakespeare"), power that is recognized and respected by those over whom one has power. Power as sheer force results only in fear and destructiveness. Power that is construed along the lines of authority already has trust built into it—trust in the boss's competence, trust in his or her identification with the good of the company, trust that he or she recognizes his or her authority rather than merely the threats of power, force, and coercion. It is in this sense that we trust our family doctors, not because they have our health in their hands but because we recognize their knowledge, authority, and concern for our well-being.

It is a mistake to think of trust as an involuntary necessity, as if one trusts only when one has no other choice. Trust backed up by Draconian sanctions is hardly trust. One might argue that even in such circumstances trust is always a choice, even if the alternative, not trusting, is sometimes limited to grudging resentment in the face of necessity. But surely this is trust in an extremely attenuated sense. Trust and the decision to trust may still be in us, even though deciding to trust in the face of force may be a desperate or a saintly act. Trust by way of authority, on the other hand, is different from—in fact, the very opposite of—forced cooperation through coercion, and obedience through fear.

For most of human history, however, it is Machiavelli whose ideas have ruled in practice. During the cold war, politics was discussed almost exclusively in terms of strategy and sheer power. One "trusted" an ally on the basis of the appropriate declarations of (tentative) allegiance and an occasional bloody display of anti-Communist zeal against the local citizenry. Politics was defined by nuclear deterrence, not trust. The dynamics of cold war relationships were characterized by military zeal and celebrated in literature and film in the images of dashing spies, counterspies, and double agents, from the very real Kim Philby to Ian Fleming's fictional James Bond and John Le Carré's semifictional spooks. In such a world, power makes sad sense as the alternative to extinction. "Better dead than red," though overstated, expressed the desperate sentiment of such a confrontation. However inspiring the gentle words of the peace movement, the idea of unilateral disarmament—the last word, perhaps, in trust—had a hard time getting situated in a world defined by the balance of power.[16]

But the destructiveness of power and fear in human affairs is obvious in the pathetic and often tragic social relations that resulted from such power politics. It was power—Soviet style—that kept Eastern Europe in darkness for years, stifling community, undermining relationships, suffocating trust, killing both commerce and civility. And, not to be too geopolitically smug, it has been power and fear—American style—that have kept in place many of the most brutal "authoritarian" regimes, particularly in the United States' own self-declared hemisphere of influence.[17] It has now been thoroughly recognized that corporations that rely on power hierarchies tend to be inefficient and often demoralizing places to work, and the women's movement (and even the backlash against the women's movement) removed the possibility of unbridled patriarchy from the majority of middle-class homes in the more advanced industrial societies.

In a culture structured by power relations, commitments and promises have a different meaning than they do in a context of mutual trust. In the former, one might expect that promises will be honored, but only because of the fear of retribution if the promise goes unfulfilled, or because the person who has failed in his or her promise will be forced to make enormous sacrifices. These two possibilities are not mutually exclusive. For example, a corrupt police officer might overlook a crime because he fears retribution against his family, but after overlooking a large number of such crimes, he may feel it necessary to continue to overlook them because his now long record of overlooking crimes will be exposed if he stops doing it. In a power-defined context, there is always an ulterior motive. In such a context, trust is self-interested calculation. Loyalty is the strategy of sticking with the stronger party. Weak people in power relationships—as Friedrich Nietzsche writes of resentful slaves—may become clever, and they almost inevitably become conspiratorial.

But self-interested calculation, cleverness, and conspiracy undermine an organization or a society. They are not virtues but destructive vices, even when—especially when—they become prudent and necessary. When the workers' main concern is avoidance of punishment for failure or the potential cost of noncompliance, the motivating force in an organization will not be cooperation—although the necessity for collaboration may make that seem to be the case. It will be suspicion and distrust, countered only by an individual's confidence in his or her ability to maneuver in, and make the best of, a bad situation. The most damaging, although nearly invisible, aspect of such a power culture is the loss of creativity. Control-minded autocrats tend to see creativity as threatening; if they miss it at all, they try to force it into existence, which inevitably fails. The essential virtue of trust is its openness, its celebration of possibilities. Force and fear shut these down. To be sure, every authoritarian regime has its occasional genius, usually an artist or writer who slips past the oppressive apparatus to produce works—almost always condemned—that get recognized only elsewhere, where the values of freedom and creativity are in place. But the usual fate of creativity, like that of freedom, is to be crushed by the forces of fear. In a power culture, people tend to see themselves as satisfying other people's demands and are far more concerned with doing so and avoiding punishment for not doing so than they are about moving the organization forward.

Consider a marriage in which one spouse is terrified of the other—whether physically or emotionally. The frightened person will come to see his or her role in the relationship almost wholly in terms of avoidance and resentment, satisfying the other's demands out of fear, never daring to make any one of the thousands of little gestures that move a romance or marriage forward and tighten the bonds of intimacy.

In all such relationships—whether in a corporation, an authoritarian community, or a marriage—people naturally feel alienated from their actions, for which they will not feel responsible except insofar as they fear punishment for failure or, in the happier case, expect some reward. And because of the inordinate emphasis placed on succeeding (or rather on not failing), there is a desperate avoidance of risks and obstacles that might increase the likelihood of failure. In a power culture, even to raise the possibility of failure—for example, by trying to explain the difficulties of a task to one's boss—is itself an indication of failure, and to be avoided.

When something does go wrong, the strong tendency is to

lie, or to shift the blame. But mistakes should not be subject to blame and punishment; they should be seen as a means to development. As Andrew Grove of Intel, one of America's most dynamic companies, told his early workers, "If you haven't made any mistakes, you're just not trying hard enough." But in power organizations and relationships the penalties for lying become even more severe than the penalties for failure; this only increases the fear and the prudence of risk avoidance. It adds to a manager's or employee's sense of responsibility only in that it increases his or her sense of vulnerability and entrapment. It makes cordial hypocrisy virtually a matter of survival.

The great advantage of a trust culture over a power culture is the ability—the need—to appreciate other people's circumstances and points of view. There is a lot of talk about "diversity" these days, but much of the discussion surrounds issues of fairness and affirmative action. These are important issues, to be sure, but they overlook the good that comes from people expressing their values and passions, each person from his or her own perspective, which leads to fruitful discussion, corrective criticism, and the emergence of a shared willingness to explore new possibilities. There is also a great deal of talk these days about being "customer-oriented" in business, but insofar as the customer remains the "object" or the "target" of marketing, such talk is wildly off the mark and self-defeating. Instead, the point should be to become familiar with the practices of the customers, with their needs and perspectives, and establish relationships in which trust, not dependence, is the definitive bond. Such trust and attention make innovation possible, and it is innovation that wins the day.

Focus has been placed on the importance of communication in marriage, but that phrase should not be understood merely to mean the routine exchange of information, or even the exchange of information about personal feelings. It is no doubt true, as much research has shown, that couples do not spend enough time talking together to share fully not only the details and grievances of their lives but their visions and concerns. But the essence is trust; the goal is to open up to each other, not so much in the expression of feelings as in the mutual appreciation and eventual sharing of feelings. Expression is not the point. Coming to share the other's outlook on life and on the relationship is much more important than airing one's affections and grievances (although obviously the one may provide the vehicle for the other). And that sharing is not mysterious; it is the making (and keeping) of commitments that both partners clearly understand.

Compare the romantic manipulations of a playboy or a coquette—someone who is clever at evoking feelings in others—with the behavior of a loving spouse. The loving spouse is probably not so clever. He or she is probably utterly without strategy. But in terms of intimacy, insight, and innovation—which means moving the relationship forward, not just introducing new little tricks and thrills—there is no comparison. The manipulative lover has power over the other, but the trust instilled is immediately undermined by betrayal.

When we attempt to control instead of respect, trust, and inspire one another, the results will always be strained and the consequences can be disastrous. As any high school teacher who is not a weight-lifting black belt in karate can tell you, keeping order with threats alone is at best a stressful and risky business. Reliance on strict laws and severe sanctions is the hallmark not of a civilized society, but of a not-yet-civil one. And, as any shop steward can tell you, maximizing efficiency with threats is ultimately bad business and encourages minimal performance and even sabotage.

Reliance on enforcement and sanctions is the death knell of a relationship, an enterprise, a society. In an intimate relationship, the use of threats signals the end of the bond. In general, power provides at best a pseudosolidarity, a false intimacy, with only the temporary appearance of shared values and cooperation. But although trust is not power, it is through trust that we can acquire the greatest power: not power over others, but something far more important—the possibility for each and all of us to realize our full potential *together*.

This is not to say that a society or a relationship of trust need totally exclude coercion and fear; sometimes the fear of enforcement is necessary in social arrangements. The "voluntary" status of contributions to the Internal Revenue Service is a case in point, and every marriage, even the most trusting, carries with it implicit threats and sanctions. But when a society or a relationship based on trust is successful, coercion and fear are all but irrelevant.

Distrust: "Paranoia" and Cynicism

Distrust is not so much the opposite as it is "the other side of" trust (as in the other side of a coin; you cannot have one side without the other). But because we so often take as our paradigm "simple trust"—trust transparent and taken for granted— it seems as if trust and distrust could not be more strongly opposed. Trust is straightforward, while distrust, for obvious reasons, tends to be devious. Trust requires some degree of mutual understanding and cooperation (even—or especially— in competitive circumstances). Distrust is adversarial, even when it is not competitive. Trust suggests the will to believe. Distrust demands suspicion. In this opposition, distrust is more dramatic. It makes a better story. It seems to be both more concrete and more convoluted than trust. It is, accordingly, the stuff of drama, whereas trust usually becomes dramatic only at those intense moments of uncertainty when distrust rears its head. But authentic trust incorporates the possibility of distrust and is inconceivable without it. Such trust is no longer "simple" but sophisticated and experienced. On the horizon of authentic trust is the penumbra of distrust, and together they define the dynamic of relationships.

In a marriage, for instance, distrust is dramatically conceived in terms of those moments of creeping horror and uncertainty: the devious, murderous spouse, the passionate, clandestine affair that has in effect already ended the marriage. But distrust infiltrates every marriage insofar as one is aware of (and grateful for) the contingencies of love and aware that love can never be guaranteed. In the contemporary world, marriages are no longer protected by social sanctions, and by their very nature they are subject to the vicissitudes of emotion and fate. To truly love someone is to live with the knowledge that his or her love cannot be taken for granted, that it is something precious and perishable. It is to realize—against the defensive limitations of your horrified imagination—that he or she *could* love another, *could* lead another life, *could* be turned against you, whether by the mischievous plottings of some cut-rate Iago or (more likely) by your own insensitivity and misdeeds. But to conclude from this that marriages (and all love relationships) are always at risk is to dwell on the negative. Love and marriage open up worlds of new possibilities precisely because they involve the mutual resolve to trust, even in the face of the most intimate and therefore the potentially most terrifying dangers.

Although we sometimes speak of "unconditional trust" (as we speak of "unconditional love"), trust (like love) almost always has its limits. An awareness of those limits is essential to trust. Beyond the limits of trust lies distrust, or at least the continuing possibility of distrust. Trust always involves risks. Betting on the outcome can be understood only in terms of an awareness of alternative outcomes.[18] But to dwell on trust as risk is to miss the main point about trust: that it opens the door to positive outcomes that would be impossible without it. Our thesis here is akin to what Dostoyevsky (and many others) have suggested concerning religious faith, that faith is not really faith unless it is punctuated, perhaps even pervaded, by doubt. But doubt is not itself the heart of faith. It is only its darker side. Faith, accordingly, is a form of self-overcoming. It is not to be thought of simply as a matter of naïve, unthinking acceptance, much less "blind" faith.

Similarly, authentic trust is not simply a matter of blind trust but a form of self-overcoming, and what must be overcome (but not therefore denied) is distrust. Naïve (or "simple") trust, trust as yet unchallenged or unquestioned (such as the faith of a well-brought-up child), might still be called trust, but that is why we carefully distinguish it from mature, "authentic" trust, which is articulated and carefully considered. Too many accounts of trust suppose that trust is merely a matter of affect or unwillingness to consider contrary arguments and evidence. Thus trust is variously described as subjective, nonevidential, blind, and irrational. But trust is (or can be) rational. It may well take into account all of the available evidence. It is not subjective so much as it is *inter*subjective—dependent on social relationships and mutual responses. In a sense, trust is not about evidence and outcomes at all, except as secondary concerns. Authentic trust is ultimately about relationships and what it takes to create, maintain, and restore them.

But to say that trust is about relationships is not to deny that the distrust to be overcome may be the product of large, impersonal social forces—for instance, the enormous pressure on families in our culture, the restructuring and increased competitiveness of many modern businesses, the multicultural confusions and confrontations of the new world order. The building of personal trust often begins with the understanding of the suprapersonal sources of distrust. In business, people may no longer feel that they understand their roles in their companies, and they may fear for their job security even when they think they have been doing a good job. The combination of competitive pressures and fear has resulted in lower morale and efficiency, as well as plummeting loyalty and dedication. Perhaps most dramatically, the flattening of many corporate hierarchies and the new emphasis on cross-functional "customer focus teams" have brought people together from different parts of those organizations, creating an unprecedented emphasis on teamwork and trust, but creating the context for pervasive distrust as well. How do we create the former while avoiding the latter? But perhaps that is not the right question. Rather, how do we incorporate distrust into an authentic form of trust? The new global economy, to take a prominent example, provides a convenient target for blame. The challenge is to understand the ways in which that economy is undermining old presuppositions and practices of trust, and to create new ones.

Trust is created and tends to be reinforced by trusting. When we trust people, we look hard for further reasons to trust them, and usually we find them. But distrust, too, has a self-creating and self-confirming nature. We all know the familiar spiral of distrust, the vendetta, that infamous cycle of escalating vengeance once endemic around the Mediterranean. The spiral of distrust may involve emotional violence more often than physical violence (although the latter may well be a consequence), but the logic of suspicion and confirmation is much like the logic of betrayal and revenge. The spiral may begin when a relationship or society experiences a whiff of mistrust for which there is some evidence, and this provokes increased diligence and suspicion, disclosing what seems to be more evidence. The distrust creates a distance, and the expression of that distrust generates a further distance, an alienation of affection, which in turn provokes resentment and often precipitates the betrayal that was feared in the first place. One betrayal inspires another, and the escalation of distrust—and of resentment and retaliation—will certainly lead to further distrust, if not to emotional or physical violence.

This is a standard plot line in theater and film, both in comedy (where the spiral is finally broken, the suspicion removed) and in tragedy (where it is not). Many of Shakespeare's plays (*Twelfth Night* and *Macbeth*, for example) contain this pattern. Alfred Hitchcock's thrillers also play on the spiral of suspicion, resolving it (sometimes implausibly) in the last minutes of the film. "Backward" and disintegrating societies provide real-life examples in the studies of anthropologists and historians; consider the portrait Francis Fukuyama borrows from Edward Banfield of a small town in southern Italy as a frightening illustration of how a low-trust society becomes incapable of the most elementary forms of communal cooperation.[19]

Both trust and distrust tend to be self-confirming, and it is easy to see why. If one person trusts another, the second person, knowing that he or she is trusted, will be more likely to be trustworthy, thus confirming the trust on the part of the first person. The psychological reward of trust is that it is gratifying to be trusted. It is also gratifying, in a more profound way, to trust. Trust indicates respect, and trust creates a bond (if only, at first, the bond of trust). The problem with thinking about trust as an attitude toward other people is that it ignores the *reciprocal* nature of trust. Most people respond to trust by being trustworthy, making further trust all the more likely. (This explains the particular animus we have toward "con artists" and others who build trust only in order to betray it. We are forgiving of those we simply do not trust. We expect nothing of them. But toward those who abuse our trust, we feel only outrage, and forgiveness is difficult.) We also interpret the evidence in such a way as to confirm that we have trusted wisely. If we trust people, we will be more likely to interpret their subsequent behavior favorably, and we will adopt that view which best supports our perception of them as trustworthy.[20]

This tendency toward self-confirmation is even more evident in the downward spiral of distrust. As soon as we distrust people, we become less likely to establish the kind of dependent or cooperative relations with them that might enable them to demonstrate their trustworthiness. We will interpret their behavior and seek out evidence of their untrustworthiness in such a way as to confirm that our caution and refusal to trust are prudent. Worse still, distrust provokes resentment, alienation, and suspicion on the part of the person mistrusted. This makes it all the more likely that the person who is not trusted will try to "rub it in," perhaps (perversely) proving himself or herself trustworthy just out of spite. (Nietzsche: "What we recognize in a person, we also inflame in him.")[21] Worse yet, he or she may make an added effort to establish himself or herself as untrustworthy, even in arenas that were previously uncontested.

The extremes of distrust are most evident in the vernacular (as opposed to clinical) notion of *paranoia,* a mental state (and in severe cases a pathological condition) in which one perceives other people as hostile and perhaps as conspiratorial.[22] In politics, in particular, such paranoia deserves special recognition. As one recent book has it, it is "the leitmotif in political life" and "the master political illness."[23] But paranoia is too often described in terms of delusion, seeing or suspecting what is not true or plausible. Such dismissive views of paranoia miss the insight of that familiar joke, "Even paranoiacs have real enemies." Paranoia need be neither a falsification nor the imposition of an implausible interpretive scheme. It may be a perfectly plausible even if self-destructive perspective on the way things really are. (It is well confirmed in the social science literature that people who have an accurate estimate of the likelihood of failure and betrayal do far less well than people who are "overly optimistic.")[24] Paranoiacs are locked into a vision that, even if true, makes a good life and flourishing human relationships impossible. So too, in corporate and organizational life, an atmosphere of paranoia guarantees waste, inefficiency, and possible sabotage. Andrew Grove, the chief executive officer of Intel, poignantly describes the anxiety and uncertainty of the high-tech market in his best-selling book, *Only the Paranoid Survive.*[25] But within the company, and between the company and its customers, such paranoia would ensure disaster. Bosses who believe that fear is an efficient motivator either do not require anything more than mere obedience from their employees or are woefully deficient in their understanding of human behavior.

This brings us to the widespread and socially sanctioned version of paranoia—*cynicism.*[26] In what we say, and increasingly in what we do, we are becoming a cynical society, a society in which an attitude of distrust is almost obligatory. A popular talk show host recently complained, "It's as if something is wrong with you if you're optimistic and feel good about things." Cynicism is a refusal to trust (and is thus different from a healthy skepticism, which says, rather, "Let's not be gullible"). If trust opens up new worlds, distrust closes them off.

Cynicism is a closed-door policy, and with its equally dark ally, resentment, it poisons ongoing possibilities as well as foreclosing new ones. Deborah Tannen has recently written that ours has become an *agonistic* society, one that encourages aggression and polarized competition when we ought to be thinking in terms of open conversation, negotiation, and compromise.[27] In business life, as in civic contexts, cynicism shuts down not only honest criticism but also hope. The assumption that things will not improve can be devastating to any growing enterprise, and although cynicism rarely leads directly to sabotage, the demoralization it carries with it often has as devastating an effect. Cynicism can shut down trust even where trust is most likely to bloom and flourish.

It has often been noted that cynicism and gullibility go

hand in hand; it has also been said that cynicism is no more than a cool façade trying to hide a raging and irrational will to believe. Both the current conversation about trust and the belief in widespread distrust are coupled with the most bizarre but widespread examples of foolish trust—for example, trust in crackpot political organizations, in equally crackpot religious movements, in motivational gurus, and in psychic hotlines. Late-night television offers an unprecedented number of get-rich-quick schemes that enrich only their creators. In Albania, a country known only for its anti-Western paranoia for most of the past half-century, the economy recently collapsed under the weight of a local pyramid scheme. Decades of cynicism about capitalism left the citizenry utterly defenseless against the oldest scam in the book. This pathological combination of foolish trust and extreme distrust (plus profound inexperience and a misunderstanding of the nature of free enterprise) led to social and economic disaster. Distrust thus weakens rather than strengthens our perspicacity and common sense in trusting, and tends to be a willing accomplice in its own worst fears.

Cordial hypocrisy feeds cynicism. In turn, it receives its rationale from cynicism. It adopts the attitude that "this is use-less; the situation will never change." This attitude promotes cordial hypocrisy as the path of least resistance. But it is also a self-fulfilling prophecy. Objections unvoiced provide no direction for improvement. Bad ideas insincerely praised lead in exactly the wrong direction. Distrust unexpressed provides no forum for building trust, because building trust requires talking about trust. Building trust requires action too, but it is mislead-ing to object that action alone is what is important to trust. True, talk without action leads only to distrust, and silent action is sometimes quite eloquent. But the essence of building trust is making commitments, and wordless commitments are rare. Indeed, making and honoring commitments involve pre-cisely the same combination of words and action that builds trust. Building trust requires talking about trust, and talking about trust—talking honestly about trust—undermines cyni-cism and leads to the dissolution of distrust.

There is always evidence to feed and confirm distrust. Trust similarly feeds and confirms trust. Because trust always involves risk, there is never any airtight proof of the wisdom of trusting. But this is not in itself a good reason for not trusting.[28] This point cannot be made too emphatically, particularly in the face of the insistence that people have to *earn* our trust. If we insist that others prove their trustworthiness *before* we trust them, our distrust, no matter how tentative, will more likely provoke the downward spiral of distrust than allow room for building trust. Trust must begin with trust.

Basic Trust

We begin by trusting. We learn to trust in infancy, and we carry that sense of trust with us throughout our lives. Thus we might begin with the conception of trust that the psychiatrist Erik Erikson called "basic trust."[29] Basic trust is basic by virtue of its foundational nature. It is an overall orientation toward the world, a set of attitudes and protopractices that are established early in childhood. Basic trust may even be, in part, inherited and innate, part of one's inborn temperament. It is evident that most infants from their first few moments are more or less trusting of the people who hold them. Others seem wary, even before it is plausible that they have any "knowledge" of what they might be wary about.[30] As we grow up, our sense of basic trust is enhanced or undermined by our experiences with other people.

If expectations are frustrated, if needs are left unfulfilled, if security is threatened or violated, a baby naturally becomes distrustful. That distrust becomes the generalized stance from which that child enters (or refuses to enter) into new relationships and situations. Worst of all are the cases of abused children, who, in their innocence, and before they have a firm grasp of what they should expect from reality, find themselves traumatized by the very caretakers with whom they need to establish basic trust. Only with great difficulty will some of them ever experience basic trust—the ability and willingness to meet people without inordinate suspicion, the ability comfortably to talk to and deal with strangers, the willingness to enter into intimate relationships. As Erikson wrote, "Some day, maybe, there will exist a well-informed, well-considered, and yet fervent public conviction that the most deadly of all possible sins is the mutilation of a child's spirit, for such mutilation undercuts the life principle of trust."

If there is an innate predisposition to trust, one might consider an evolutionary explanation; given the gross social and individual disadvantages of widespread distrust and the propensity for mutual damage among creatures who do not trust one another, natural selection would have favored those who trust and cooperate over those who do not. This point is often made by sociobiologists regarding the evolution of altruism, but similar considerations suffice for an analysis of the evolution of trust. Social evolution would have further selected for the same features, eliminating those who betray and break their trust and encouraging the others to trust. Robert Axelrod's computer-generated "tit-for-tat" model of cooperation suggests on a strictly strategic basis that there is a distinct evolutionary advantage to the presumption of trust combined with a willingness (or a felt need) to retaliate in response to betrayal.[31] Babies are too weak and uncoordinated to retaliate, but one does not have to search far to find infantile equivalents (screaming, refusing to eat, throwing food on the floor, and the like).

Basic trust provides the basis for one's entire personality and demeanor toward the world. It concerns not only physical security and needs but also what R.D. Laing has called "ontological security,"[32] security in one's own being and one's place in the world. Some developmental psychologists have created a working hypothesis regarding the social expectations of the infant, which become more sophisticated with experience as he or she becomes a child, then an adolescent.[33] The working model changes with time, but the basic shape is established early. As a child learns to trust, he or she develops a set of practices and approaches concerning basic security, basic needs, and the basic satisfactions of life, a generalized paradigm of hopes, fears, expectations, and entitlements. But the family is the basis of not only simple trust—trust based on familiarity and taken for granted—but authentic trust, trust that is focused on relationships rather than single transactions and outcomes.

The trust that originates in families may or may not be coupled with a complementary tendency to distrust those who are not one's family. This tendency defines what Fukuyama calls "low-trust societies," societies in which the family is to be trusted and others are not. But beyond the family, it is clear that trust must be learned—first of all from the attitudes of one's family. A distrustful family will tend to raise distrustful children. One may learn over time—or over generations—that other families are not to be trusted. Or one may learn this through the following sort of inference: Edward Banfield, in his study of southern Italy, notes that the "reasoning" here is that one knows that one is greatly favoring one's own family and thereby infers that others in other families do likewise.[34]

But although the notion of "blood" reigns in such situations (it is worth noting which societies place a high premium on blood relations and which do not), one's sense of family does not depend on blood, genes, or any other straightforward biological knowledge. Here the concept of familiarity takes on a literal and seminal significance. It is the family, first of all, that is familiar and the basis for all further familiarities. Fukuyama's diagnosis of low-trust societies suggests that, in most societies, trust is correlated with the familiar, distrust with the unfamiliar. Advanced industrial societies may discourage extended families, but they famously encourage the sorts of artificial communities and mediating associations that Fukuyama celebrates as the key to high-trust and prosperous societies.[35]

By its nature, basic trust is relatively open-ended and indiscriminate. Basic trust can thus be equated with what Bernard Barber calls "basic trust in the moral social order."[36] In one sense, the structure of basic trust is largely negative; it is trust that bad things will not happen. Basic trust is the trust people have, walking down the streets of their neighborhoods, that they will not be assaulted or insulted. Insofar as the trust is basic, and not the product of martial arts training, a police escort, or much-studied safety maps of the area, the threat of assault is not even considered. The street feels safe because it feels familiar. The infinity of bad things that could possibly happen while walking down our own streets is for most of us relegated to *Halloween*-type movies and stand-up comedy. The horror of Sarajevo, by contrast, was not just the brutality of ethnic war. It was that this famously congenial multicultural community turned virtually overnight from familiar neighborhoods into a dangerous and anxiety-provoking landscape in which even a walk down one's own street became a matter of incomprehensible terror.

Without basic trust and the routine justification of that trust, life would be terrifying indeed. Unfortunately, nearly a fifth of the population of the United States, and a much larger proportion of the people of the third world, do not have such trust and have no reason to have it. President Woodrow Wilson famously urged America (on its entrance into the First World War) to "make the world safe for democracy." But in order to do this, it is necessary to make the world safer for basic trust.

Trusting Strangers: The Global Society

Basic trust may provide the psychological and cultural foundation for trust, but it ought not to be conflated with authentic trust, the sort of trust that is the product of experience, resolve, and commitments. It may be perfectly "natural" that we tend to feel more comfortable with people we know and others who seem like "our own," who may be unknown to us but are not "strange." But in the world today trust cannot be limited to those we know, and Fukuyama is surely right that low-trust societies tend to shut themselves out of the cooperative alliances that make prosperity possible in the modern world.

It is by no means a matter of simple prejudice that people tend to distrust people who are different from themselves, but civilization has always required the accommodation and acceptance of strangers. (The ancient Greeks considered themselves a "civilized" society—and set the standard for Western society—precisely because they insisted on the proper treatment of strangers. In ancient Asia, Confucius established much the same standard.)

Familiarity is naturally the first step beyond family; it involves the sense of a relationship already formed. Thus trust is easiest and most natural with those we know, with whom trust is already established. But our world is no longer a world of tribal families and those who are familiar. Most of us no longer live or work with, or even near, our parents and childhood friends. Marriages are more likely to be between people from different cities than with "the boy or girl next door." Strangers become intimates much more readily now than they did when preferences were restricted to tribal and village neighbors. Intimate friendships and important alliances are struck up over drinks or coffee. Romances are kindled on commuter trains and the Internet. Couples who divorce suddenly find themselves facing a new and often alien world in which they need to build trust with strangers.

We drive on highways and along streets surrounded by strangers. Business deals are made in casual conversations on golf links and in bowling alleys. Corporate managers are moved with their families across the country. We switch jobs as the need or opportunity arises, putting our lives in the hands of people we know (at best) only by reputation or on the basis of an interview or letter. Most of us live in cities populated by strangers. We shop in stores where our most intimate connection with the salesperson on the other side of the counter comes when we hand over our credit cards. More and more shopping is done not at the corner store, but on the World Wide Web, with people and companies we will never see. Farmers in Iowa now must find customers in Asia, and even the most cautious consumer now buys products from unseen strangers on the Internet. International alliances are now prevalent, not only among huge multinational corporations but also among small companies, people in all walks of life, and nongovernment organizations.

In our day-to-day lives, we are surrounded by strangers whom we implicitly trust *because we have to*. We are people on the move. We are citizens of and consumers in a global society.

We meet and work with strangers all the time. And more often than we may notice, we trust complete strangers to be fair, honest, and reasonable in their dealings with us. We trust them to do what they have said they will do, or what they can reasonably be expected to do. When they do not do so, we feel outraged or betrayed. But most of the time, people do what they are expected to do, not because they have to or feel compelled to, but because they know (without being conscious that they know) that they too are participants in a network of trust. Life would be unlivable if we were not part of this network. Life, growth, and happiness are possible only insofar as we trust. We trust in part because of protective devices (such as encryption codes in computer credit card transactions), references, reputations, and brand names. But without trust, there would be no business, and without trust between strangers, there would be no global (or for that matter, even regional) economy.

Business, personal relationships, and politics have always required trust. But what makes our era different is that our need to trust strangers is increasing exponentially. It once was the case that most of our business—and the sum of our social transactions—could take place within the local community. New technology means that new worlds appear all the time, and those who want to "stay on top of things" need trust not only in the technology but in themselves and in the new world that is being created. Survival, contra Andrew Grove, demands not paranoia but its opposite—cooperation and coordination, both of which require trust.

The fast pace of this new world makes it difficult for us to take the time to get to know each other. Familiarity, in that familiar sense, is neither possible nor necessary on a grand scale. Companies that cannot establish trust quickly will not be able to compete. And the business of the future—indeed, the business of the present—depends on a network of trust virtually devoid of personal histories and relationships. The obvious exceptions are those who become renowned for shady dealings and broken promises. In the new world of trust, it is easy to become instantly known as someone *not* to be trusted, while building trust may take many customers, many transactions, and many commitments and expectations fulfilled. In the absence of familiarity, nothing is more important than a good—even impeccable—reputation.

The new need for trust is leaving many of our old institutions behind, in part because the power and hierarchy that characterize them are too often institutionalized forms of distrust. "Management," in most of its incarnations, is an institutionalized form of distrust. For that reason, many of today's managers are increasingly ill suited to assume leadership roles in a fast-changing world. Companies that institutionalize distrust move too slowly to compete, and they lose out on the opportunities that only trust can open. To trust is to take a risk, and risks should be taken wisely. But to trust is also *to open new worlds*.

If we think of trust primarily in terms of vulnerability, it will seem foolish, a weakness rather than a strength, a liability rather than an asset. But once we think of trust as an opening, as a foundation for new and perhaps unimagined possibilities, then trust takes on a different appearance. Trusting strangers becomes the very heart of wisdom, strength rather than foolishness, a promising investment in the future rather than a liability. The cost of trust may on occasion be devastating, but the high cost of distrust is virtually guaranteed.

Talking about Trust

Building trust, we suggest, begins with talk about trust—talk combined with action, to be sure, but talk first of all. We are creatures who talk, and therefore we are thinking, reflective creatures. We don't just avow our trust, we examine it, and we can thereby create and build it.

Unfortunately, discussions of trust as an unmitigated good tend to be banal and devoid of content. Really talking about trust is discomforting. In business, executives heartily express their approval—"Yes, we need more trust" (perhaps because in many corporations trust is at an all-time low)—but then they nervously turn to other topics. Couples acknowledge the need for trust and the joy of trusting, but then they shyly avoid opening up those areas where trust really is in question. Better to "simply trust one another" than to talk about such matters.

Talking about trust unavoidably suggests that one ought to *do* something. Accordingly, we prefer to *simulate* talk about trust, using the word but really engaging in cordial hypocrisy or a conversation of blame and lament: "How can I trust him when he is so untrustworthy?" "Why doesn't anyone trust anyone else anymore?" Or, having said a few good words about trust, we think that the subject has been covered. After all, if one trusts, then nothing more need be said, and it is much better that nothing be said. Even to raise the question "Do you trust me?" or "Can I trust you?" not only indicates distrust—it actually instigates distrust. If one does not trust, then nothing much is accomplished by saying so, except perhaps the escalation of an already existing conflict, or the offering of an insult or a confirming test ("If you tell me that I should trust you, then you are doubly a liar"). A politician or a leader who says "Trust me" takes a considerable risk. Supporters may well wonder why this needs to be said, and become suspicious. For those who are already suspicious, such an imperative only confirms their suspicions.[37]

Talk about trust, much like talk about love, is tantalizingly paradoxical. The French aphorist François La Rochefoucauld insightfully suggested that few people would ever have fallen in love had they never heard the word. Love is, in part, a linguistic phenomenon, a language-created emotional relationship. There are all sorts of emotional attachments among all sorts of creatures, including infant human beings, who do not use language. But talking about love, weaving stories about love, confessing to love, are actions that do not merely comment on our feelings but, to a significant extent, create and shape them. "I love you" is not so much a description of a feeling as it is a provocative act, inviting or demanding a change in a relationship, moving it either forward toward romance or backward toward discomfort and disintegration.

So too, "I trust you" is not merely a description but a creative act, intended to manipulate or reassure another person. In addition, when someone says "I trust you," the statement can impose an unwanted psychological burden whose consequences may well be guilt and resentment. "I don't trust you" is never simply a description of a psychological state. Either it is an important step in moving an untrusting relationship toward the sorts of commitment and attention that would make it a trusting one, or it is a way of breaking off the relationship. "Don't trust me" is an act of sublime mischief, a way of waving off responsibility; but it is also deeply paradoxical. ("Why should I trust your instruction not to trust you?") "Trust me" is the performative linchpin of trust, implied in every promise, in every assurance, in every declaration, in every statement whatsoever. ("Trust that what I say is true.") But its being implied also tends to make it sound superfluous or suspicious when someone actually makes a point of saying it.

In the movie *Blaze,* stripper Blaze Starr's mother wisely warns her (at the start of her long, scandalous relationship with Governor Huey Long of Louisiana), "Don't trust any man who says, 'Trust me.'" The film is set in the 1940s, but it reflects an attitude that is still prevalent. In a good marriage, for example, "trust me" is either superfluous or an intimation of hard times ahead. In an ordinary business deal, it could be an indication of a con job or a polite but unnecessary assurance, for without trust the arrangement would not have proceeded in the first place.

We all know the importance and advantages of trust, and we all know how terrible life can be without it. But when it comes time to put that knowledge into practice, we are like the novice skydiver who, having eagerly read all of the promotional literature about the thrills of the sport and having listened carefully to instructions, then asked incredulously, "But now you want us to *jump out of the plane?*"

To trust is to take on the personal responsibility of making a commitment and choosing a course of action, and with it, one kind of relationship or another. Trust entails a lack of control, but it means entering into a relationship in which control is no longer the issue. There is no need to broach the subject of trust with people or things that we can utterly control.

Trust may seem to be a leap from the dark plane of our ordinary cynicism into the unsupported free fall of dependency. But we torture ourselves with false ideas of dependency when what trust makes possible is an eminently more effective *inter*dependency: cooperation and the expansion of possibilities. It is always, to some extent, what the Danish philosopher Søren Kierkegaard famously called "a leap of faith." And yet nothing is more necessary than the leap into trust. That leap can be initiated by learning to talk about trust, and by making promises and commitments that command trust, put it into practice, and make it fully explicit. As Kierkegaard also noted, what we create through our vulnerability is the solid security of a relationship.

Talking about trust is not so much a matter of "Do we or don't we?" or "Should we or shouldn't we?" as of "How will we?" This is not to deny that trusting someone, particularly in the light of accusatory evidence, or a history of treachery and deceit, is difficult indeed. It is not to say that Palestinians and Israelis, Bosnian Serbs and Muslims, bankers and their bankrupt clients, and spouses rushing toward divorce can simply will their past, their fears, and their suspicions away. Nevertheless, talking about trust and believing that trust is possible— even in the face of extreme and vehement distrust—is the first and essential step. Talk may begin with venom and mutual accusations, but accusations that are well intentioned or well mediated can lead to negotiations, and negotiations can then lead to mutual commitments, small at first, which build trust. Mutual commitments and their fulfillment may never put an end to distrust, but they do build trust—authentic trust, trust with its eyes wide open.

Authentic trust is a judicious combination of trust and distrust, superior to blind trust, which is foolish precisely because it bars distrust from consideration. But to talk about trust is to recognize, first and foremost, that we are (like it or not) in this together, whether "this" is a marriage, a business relationship, a corporation, a community, a continent, or the world. A trusting relationship, no matter how tentative, is always better than war.

Building Trust

Building trust requires talking and thinking about trust. If we get stuck on the idea that all trust should be like basic trust, primal, unthinking, devoid of doubt, then we will never get to authentic trust. If we get caught in the paradigm of trust as familiarity (marriage, friendship, a long-standing partnership), we will never envision a paradigm that includes building trust among strangers. But talking and thinking about trust, whether within intimate relationships, within a corporation, or between strangers in a global transaction, is not enough. Building trust begins with an appreciation and understanding of trust, but it also requires practice and practices. Without the practices, the appreciation and understanding come to nothing. What is required is the institutionalization of trust, whether in the day-to-day rituals of a marriage or the well-organized routines of a global corporation.

In the mid-1990s the famously fractured United States Congress conducted a much-publicized retreat in Hershey, Pennsylvania, with the goal of producing civility, bipartisan cooperation, and trust. The representatives expressed great enthusiasm and high praise for the way they interacted with one another during the retreat. There were tears, hugs, expressions of camaraderie, resolutions to reform their ways. In spite of what came to be known as the "spirit of Hershey," however, the retreat was immediately followed by some of the bitterest partisan battles in years. Congress remained inefficient, ineffective, and uncivil in the extreme. Important legislation languished and died, and the internecine battles culminated in the Clinton impeachment, where the vote split along party lines, paralyzing the federal government for almost a year. During that same period, Congress conducted another retreat—again, highly successful, according to participants, but producing no discernible difference in the day-to-day conduct of business. These are the questions regarding the building of trust: How can we carry what we know about trust into the heart of a relationship or an organization? How can we create and maintain a culture of trust? And how can we create that trust between strangers that Fukuyama defines as "spontaneous sociability," trust beyond the bounds of familiarity?

Fukuyama is concerned primarily with the differences among cultures, particularly those that encourage and support such extrafamily alliances (Japan, the United States, Germany) and those that do not (China, Italy, France). We are more concerned with the challenge of change, not so much in cultures as in relationships and corporations. One might challenge Fukuyama's claims regarding some cultures (for instance, in the light of Japan's recent banking collapse and Hong Kong's remarkable success), but what is important is his insistence that economics is only a "superstructure" built on a base of culture (reversing the old Marxist architectonic, shared by almost all economists). Moving the discussion of global prosperity into the realm of culture with a specific emphasis on trust is an enormous step forward. But from culture it is necessary to move into the realm of relationships, and from the given structure of cultures to the creative nature of relationships and organizations. It may have been a mistake for Fukuyama to focus his attention on large-scale organizations rather than on the more diverse phenomena of interpersonal trust, but at least the spotlight has been moved away from the inexplicable "magic of the market" or the mysteries of "global market forces" to the concrete realm of human relationships.

Culture and human relationships are not amorphous blobs of customs and habits. They have and require structures, regular practices, the give-and-take of requests, demands, and commitments. Every society has had its periods of extreme distrust, paranoia, and internal hostility. We have had the horrors of our own Civil War, including the bitter aftermath, which many Southerners have neither forgotten nor forgiven. Most societies—those that survive—move on and learn to trust again. Aside from pockets of fanaticism and intolerance, our North-South conflict has shifted to the gentler realms of irony and sports competitions. Reestablishing trust means establishing new structures, restoring regular practices, reinstituting interactions. Television, mobility, fast communications, business interests, and now the Internet have replaced the old, local loyalties with national and international concerns. (There is at least a hint of racism in the suggestion that some societies are hopeless cases while others are blessed with civic virtue and prosperity.) Trust in a society is not a given. It is the product of collective, self-conscious action.

Building trust is no longer a matter of creating structures and practices within a single culture. Global trust has come to the fore, and no single culture or its practices can define the nature of trust. Moreover, from a global perspective, it is more evident than ever that building trust cannot be a matter of implementation from above—although the example of world and local leaders and role models is always effective. Trust is built step by step, commitment by commitment, on every level. Peace between Israelis and Palestinians, or between the Catholic and Protestant Irish, will not be solidified by top-level agreements, no matter how pervasive or well enforced. Peace comes with trust, which will grow from continuing efforts toward mutual understanding and trade, Romeo-and-Juliet-style marriages, conversations, negotiations, and individual commitments. In Bosnia and in Kosovo, we have seen the sham of high-level agreements alone.

The collective result of such conversations, negotiations, and commitments is the ongoing dynamic that we call "culture" (and, on a larger scale, "civilization"). Definitions of culture typically emphasize shared values, rituals, and beliefs, but what really defines a culture—or a multicultural civilization—is trust. It is true, as the Greeks were fond of pointing out, that how people behave and whether or not they trust one another has a great deal to do with the overall culture and climate of a society. But at the same time, culture and climate are the products of trust, and trust cannot be established simply by fiat. Trust must be built one step (sometimes it seems like a giant step indeed) at a time, by way of interpersonal confrontations and mutual engagements, by way of commitments and promises, offers and requests.

Building trust means thinking about trust in a positive way. If trust is considered only in terms of risks and vulnerabilities, no incentive is provided. True, trust necessarily carries with it uncertainties, but we must force ourselves to think about these uncertainties as possibilities and opportunities, not as liabilities. This means trusting trust, which means in turn trusting ourselves. Too many philosophers have analyzed trust in terms of knowledge and beliefs—that is, as a set of probability calculations, based on knowledge of the payoffs and punishments—or in terms of keeping one's commitments versus betraying them, the character and track record of the trusted person, and so on. But this approach too readily leads to a magnified emphasis on risk and a limited palette of choices. Trust opens up new and unimagined possibilities. Trust is not bound up with knowledge so much as it is with freedom, the openness to the unknown. This means moving beyond the realm of Knowing What We Know to the richer realm of Knowing What We Do Not Know, and the even richer realm and the exciting opportunities of learning What We Do Not Even Know That We Do Not Know. This is not a realm that most of us can enter alone. We can arrive there only with and through other people. And for that, we have to trust them.

In the realm of business, the new possibilities of trust are disclosed in particular through entrepreneurship. In the business literature, entrepreneurship is the favorite name for the spark that creates new businesses and makes them grow. But entrepreneurship isn't just inventiveness. It is not just the creation of new ideas. Entrepreneurship is first of all a way of creating and participating in networks of trust. Steven Jobs, one of the young partners who founded Apple and started the personal computer revolution, did not so much invent something as create a new world in which people came to trust a formerly exotic technology and incorporate it into their lives, their jobs, and their sense of identity. Trust in such a technology does not mean merely finding a machine reliable. It means trusting the whole new and as yet unknown world of social relations into which the technology brings us.

Jobs and his partner Steve Wozniak created more than a personal computer. They shifted the entire paradigm of computing from an inaccessible, mysterious world staffed by experts in lab coats to a world full of useful and comprehensible tools and

toys that can be played with by almost anyone. Without consciously doing so, they also revolutionized the organization of
offices, the role of secretaries, the task of doing one's own typing, the way small businesses work, and, as we now see, the very
ways business is conducted. Apple, even in its current dimin-
ished role, still provides the best example of entrepreneurship
in our time. But to say that companies must learn to be entrepreneurial—one of the mantras of management consulting
these days—is to insist not that people be independent inven-
tors but that they need to work to develop bonds of trust both
internal and external to the organization. That is the true path
to innovation in the global economy.

Corporations can provide paradigms of the new trust: intimate and extensive bonds of trust created de novo for the most
part between strangers who need to establish cooperation and
collective single-mindedness. Or they can be throwbacks to
the Jurassic period of management, in which power and control, not trust, were the operational constants. But in the new
millennium, distrust will be fatal, while the risks and costs of
trust will become a routine part of doing business.

2

UNDERSTANDING AND MISUNDERSTANDING TRUST

As Nietzsche famously pointed out, that which is closest to us is often furthest from our awareness. We might think of this as a kind of blindness, an inability or unwillingness to see what is right in front of our eyes. Many people are blind to trust, not so much to its benefits as to its nature and the practices that make it possible. Indeed, these practices tend to be invisible, and trust seems to most people, most of the time, so transparent, so simple, so natural, so unproblematic—except for those special, awful occasions and situations when we are betrayed—that there is nothing much to notice, much less to understand. Either we trust someone or we do not. If people are trustworthy, we trust them. If they are not, we do not. And if we trust them, we do so unthinkingly. Indeed, to wonder is to worry, which is *not* to trust.

But such blindness can be dangerous, blocking our view of and consequently our willingness to engage in genuine, authentic trust. It leads to misunderstandings of trust, and worse, to practices that cultivate distrust. Getting beyond such blindness often brings revelatory results, in particular, a willingness to build trust where there is none, or to reestablish trust where it has already been disappointed or betrayed.

How We Misunderstand Trust

We tend to think of trust as naïve or *simple*. We think of trust as untroubled, unthinking, taken for granted, like the trust young children have for their parents. When such trust is betrayed, it cannot be restored. In this, it is much like first love, that innocent crush that precedes all knowledge and wisdom in love. But first love is not true love, and naïve trust is not authentic trust. Authentic trust requires wisdom, not naïveté.

At times we confuse trust with *blind trust,* the refusal even to consider any evidence or argument that one should not be so trusting, or that one should qualify one's trust. The sort of trust demanded by religious cult leaders and some corporate bosses is blind trust (although they are rarely so blind in their trust in their followers). Sometimes, blind trust is a response to distrust, a leap to the opposite extreme, from "I don't trust you" to "I will trust everything you say and do." This tendency to go from distrust to blind faith sometimes makes a fascinating psychological study, but all too often it simply betrays gullibility or the lack of adequate self-conception or resolute values. It is difficult to live with either distrust or the contingencies and conditions of trusting, but manufacturing unconditional trust in their stead is not necessarily a virtue.

The uncritical thought that trust is *unconditional* may be fallout from the way we talk about trust. We rarely limit our trust to such specifics as "trusting Sam to do the dishes before nine o'clock." More often we say, "I trust you," or "I trust Jim," or "I trust the company." No qualification or limitation is specified. But we should distinguish between what we explicitly say ("I trust you") and what is conversationally and situationally implied. We do not usually need to add, "of course, that doesn't mean I would trust you to perform brain surgery." Trust may seem unconditional because it tends to be open-ended and is only sometimes restricted to a single task or commitment. Nevertheless, trust is almost always conditional, focused, qualified, and therefore limited. Forgetting this can be like signing a blank check, promising anything to anyone, and thereby setting oneself up for exploitation and betrayal. In this sense, unconditional trust is just another version of blind trust.

There is another sense of unconditional trust, however, that is much more authentic, and that is a committed openness rather than a mere lack of discrimination. To trust someone is not to say "anything goes" but rather to keep open one's responses, expectations, and a willingness to negotiate. There is no particular obstacle, disappointment, or betrayal that will bring such trust to an end, because that kind of trust is dedicated to a relationship, cause, or practice that is itself open-ended—for example, making one's marriage work or creating peace in the world. But this is hardly the same as that indiscriminate trust that often is called by that name.

We also confuse trust with *familiarity*. But as we have noted, familiarity can no longer be a necessary condition for trust. Just as important, it is not a sufficient condition either. Feeling familiar may provide grounds for trust, but it can never alone warrant trust. We all make the mistake of thinking that someone is trustworthy because he or she feels familiar to us, because he or she has "been around for a while." Con artists know how to make themselves familiar while they prepare to rob you of all you are worth. Familiarity is not sufficient reason to suppose that anyone actually cares about you or shares your values. Familiarity says nothing about whether a person is sincere or trustworthy. Moreover, familiarity is no assurance of competence. Just because someone is familiar in a role does not mean that he or she is any good in that role. Your familiar doctor, despite his or her charming and comfortable bedside manner, may nevertheless be a quack. The car mechanic you know from buying gas every week may be incompetent. Your best friend may well be your worst choice for professional help and advice. In business, in particular, one learns that familiarity is often a bad basis for trust.

We also tend to mechanize trust. In other words, we confuse it with *reliance* and *dependability,* the virtues of a good machine. But trust is not a matter of predictability and expectations. It necessarily involves interactions and relationships (no matter how abbreviated). It is a function of our active commitments, which in turn assume the mode of reciprocity. Trust involves doing, not just believing; reciprocal action, not passive reliance and prediction. Trust is a mode of interpersonal engagement, not mere calculation.

We also too easily conflate *trust* and *trustworthiness,* as if these are simply two different words for the same phenomenon, two sides of the same coin. In a sense this is true, but it too readily slips into the assumption that the only sound reason for trusting someone is that he or she is trustworthy. We similarly tend to assume that someone is trustworthy if and only if he or she can be trusted. But we should not assume that a trusting relationship involves trust and trustworthiness on both sides. If we make that assumption, we oversimplify an enormously rich and subtle relationship. To put the matter crudely, we can with good reason trust someone who is not trustworthy (for example, a child who is just developing skills and responsibility), and we can with good reason refuse to trust someone who is trustworthy (for example, if there is a special reason to carry out the task ourselves). In trust, as in love, relationships are often unequal and asymmetrical, with one person trusting much more than the other does. The relationship between trust and trustworthiness is in every case "dialectical"—that is, dynamic and mutually defining.

Philosophers and jurists often think of trust in terms of *keeping one's promises.* But this is too restricted. We have and make many commitments that are not based on explicit promises. Trust is often implicit. It may be based on an explicit assessment, an evaluation of a person's prospects that is fully articulated and communicated; but it may also follow from a merely implicit assessment or simply a "transparent" way of being. We put ourselves into trusting relationships all the time, often without promising anything to anyone.

We too easily confuse *prudence* with trust. Trust may be prudent, and trust usually does, in the long run, bring the best results. But trust is not, at its root, self-interested; much less is it selfish. Calculated trust, trust that relies only on a game-theoretical matrix of advantages and outcomes, is not trust. Trust, like all virtues, has a strong element of being "good for its own sake." But like all virtues, it generally turns out to be good in its consequences. Two spouses trust each other not in order to get what they can out of the marriage but because to be happily married is to trust. A marriage based on self-interested calculation is a marriage doomed to trouble. In business as well, trust based only on calculated advantage quickly turns into bureaucratic control, suspicion, defensiveness, and mere cleverness. This diminishes flexibility and speed, and it also hampers customer relations, compromises values, and produces enormous waste, especially in enforcement costs.

Trusting does not mean following *rules.* In the 1960s, a popular slogan among people in their twenties was, "Don't trust anyone over thirty." (When the majority of fans of this maxim lived past that limit, the rule obviously had to be changed.) Parents tell their children, "Don't talk to strangers," and many adults follow the rule, "Don't trust anyone you don't know." But trust is first of all an openness, a flexible practice based on judgment, particular to each relationship, often regardless of general policies. We have noted that engineers and "scientific" managers, in particular, want to make trust into a rule along the lines of "Always investigate whether people are trustworthy." They treat people as mechanisms, as predictable followers of rules. But human beings are not mechanisms, and although they certainly are rule-following animals, the role of rules in human relationships has often been overplayed at the cost of creativity and freedom, including such essential freedoms as the freedom to be perverse, the freedom to be unpredictable, the freedom to change one's mind, and the freedom to betray those who trust one. How one trusts people has at least as much to do with the particular relationship as it does with the rules of human behavior.

Again, contrary to many recent writings on the topic, trust is not a medium, an atmosphere, a social lubricant, or glue. Trust is not a *thing,* or, for that matter, what Georg Wilhelm Friedrich Hegel referred to as a "substance," if by that expression we deny the dynamism and vitality of trust. Trust is an open-ended set of practices and activities and the interaction—not the "stuff"—of active relationships. But why trust so easily seems to be a passive connection, rather than the product of dynamic interaction and communication, is itself an important piece of the picture. We suggest that it has to do with the way trust recedes into the background of relationships. But this is not to say that trust becomes some kind of mysterious medium.

Trust is not a *feeling.* And yet, because it so clearly evokes a range of emotions, moods, and affections, we may think of trust as a feeling, a barely detectable state of mind, a calm sense of comfort, a soft affection. But there is no feeling of trust as such, and reducing trust to a feeling ignores the interactive and dynamic aspects of trust in favor of a more or less passive "intuition." Often in practice, though not in theory or on reflection, people believe that they trust others merely because they like them, or have a "good feeling" about them. We often say "I feel as if I can trust so-and-so," but this only means "I think I have reasons for trusting so-and-so" and not "I have a distinctive feeling" (as one might have a headache or an experience of anxiety). Perhaps trust can be described, in part, in terms of the absence of such feelings as anxiety and trepidation, and thus as a feeling of calm, but trust itself is not a distinctive feature of our phenomenal (feeling) life. Nevertheless, trust is inextricably involved with our emotions and moods.

Trust must again be distinguished from what we call cordial hypocrisy, that familiar façade of goodwill and congeniality that hides distrust and cynicism. The superficial and often tight-lipped smile of cordial hypocrisy may seem to support group harmony or teamwork, but it is destructive to both. Cordial hypocrisy is especially problematic in institutional settings such as work groups and corporations, but it is also painfully familiar in troubled marriages that are held together by the now thinned fibers of habit, convenience, and mere courtesy. But when we pretend that we trust even if we believe that we are trusting and trustworthy, we withhold critical information and shut down communication. Whether this is out of fear of hurting feelings, fear of getting into an argument, fear for our jobs, or fear for our marriages, we risk losing more than we salvage. We prefer to take the safe, polite route rather than to explore a riskier honesty. But politeness often hides real problems that poison relationships, while the harm done by honest disclosure is often brief and limited.

Institutions often encourage such cordial hypocrisy, supposedly in order to maintain harmony and minimize friction. The result is just the opposite, and tends to blind institutions to their institutionalization of *distrust*. Denial, not distrust, is perhaps the greatest enemy of trust.

In contrast to these various (mis)conceptions of trust, we want to defend a conception of *authentic trust,* trust that is fully self-aware, cognizant of its own conditions and limitations, open to new and even unimagined possibilities, based on choice and responsibility rather than the mechanical operations of predictability, reliance, and rigid rule-following. To be sure, promises and commitments play a central role in authentic trust, and although we distinguish trust from prudence, this is not to deny that the most prudent course of action is usually the trusting one. Authentic trust is not a matter of feeling, but it is an emotional phenomenon, involving emotional skills. It is frank, even blunt, and nothing is more alien to it than cordial hypocrisy and denial, the mere appearance of trust, or blind trust, which is to authentic trust as a forgery (not merely a reproduction) is to the original painting.

Simple Trust

Thucydides, describing moral disintegration in the late fifth century B.C., wrote, "There was every kind of wickedness afoot throughout all Greece by the occasion of civil wars. Simplicity, which is the chief cause of a generous spirit, was laughed down and disappeared. Citizens were sharply divided into opposing camps, and, without trust, their thoughts were in battle array."[38]

Thucydides is describing the tragic loss of simple trust, the unthinking emotional attitude we would all like to assume regarding our fellow citizens and which we hope we can take for granted with our friends and family. Simple trust is the kind of trust that most of us, most of the time, take as our paradigm. It consists primarily of basic trust, unthinking trust in our essential security, in the benign indifference if not the benevolence of our fellow citizens, in their respect for our rights and the fulfillment of our needs. But all these features of basic trust can rise to full consciousness when we are in a strange or dangerous situation, when we are away from our usual comfortable circumstances. Basic trust is basic insofar as it usually begins without thought or reflection and provides a general orientation to the world. But simple trust is trust that *remains* unthinking and unreflective. It is trust devoid of any sense of the possibility of distrust, trust as unthinking acceptance. One might say that it is trust by default, except that it is what most people seem to confuse with trust *as such*. Simple trust is the utter absence of suspicion. It is trust that demands no reflection, no conscious choice, no scrutiny, no justification. It may come about because no reason has ever arisen to question the other's trustworthiness, but it may also be that the one who trusts is simply naïve. It is the naïveté of trust and the utter absence of distrust that make simple trust so simple.

The paradigm of simple trust is the trust that infants have for their primary caretakers.[39] This is also the source of basic trust, but basic trust is only an orientation, the psychological core of trust, which then gets reflected in any number of more sophisticated and developed practices and responses. Simple trust, however, is nothing more than that—simple, unthinking acceptance. But even a baby's trust is not so simple. A baby's trust only seems simple because it is not and cannot yet be articulated or reflected upon, and its expressions are extremely limited. (This is why Lawrence Becker puts so much emphasis on the "noncognitive" nature of trust, but by doing so, he all but rules out articulate and therefore authentic trust from consideration.)[40] Even before babies can talk, they make it quite clear that their trust is not mere acceptance, that it is riddled with fears and suspicions, that their trust is not to be taken for granted but must be earned, virtually every time they are handled. As soon as babies have muscular control, they start testing their parents, turning their heads away, squirming, crying, throwing pacifiers or food on the floor. (Does any parent wonder why?)

Simple trust is trust that is taken for granted, that has gone unchallenged and untested, trust that is undisturbed. It is an attitude of assumption, trust by default, not a decision by way of deliberation and ethical and evidential considerations. One trusts unthinkingly. One "finds oneself" trusting. Simple trust might thus be viewed as a focused optimism. (Cornell philosopher Karen Jones wonders whether there might also be a "simple" [uncritical] form of distrust.[41] If simple trust is a kind of naïve optimism, could simple distrust be a kind of naïve pessimism?) But even if there were an innate infantile optimism, it would still fall short of the simplicity that our romance of innocence requires of the newborn. Simple trust is a sort of fantasy, and the supposed innocence of babies is its paradigm case. It is trust taken for granted, untroubled, untested, unthought of, trust as total innocence, trust as an utterly transparent ideal. Unfortunately, such trust rarely exists, even as an ideal. The supposedly transparent ideal tends to cloud our vision, for trust is rarely if ever so simple. All too often simple trust turns out to be nothing but false comfort in a situation that, if tested, proves not to be deserving of trust at all.

Some people say that trusting (simply) is "human nature." But this is to dismiss the possibility of serious inquiry. People do not "naturally" trust one another, even if, given the extreme vulnerability of infancy, in the beginning we have to trust others, at least for a while. And given the continuing vulnerability of human beings, some semblance of infantile trust remains a possibility throughout our lives, in illness, in old age, and in times of change, stress, and "helplessness." Sometimes we trust because we have no choice, and a combination of necessity and self-deception conspires to allow us to put the question of trusting out of mind, to accept what we cannot challenge or change. People who are engaged in attention-demanding, skilled activities (or who are relaxed and trying to put all worries "out of mind") also push questions of trust into the background, refusing to think about them, simply assuming what they have no time or desire to establish or resolve. Paying attention to trust, allowing for the thoughts that lead to distrust, can be distracting and upsetting. Quite understandably, we prefer not to entertain them, and this, phenomenologically, may result in simple trust, a form of naïveté. But usually, simple trust is simply inattention, a taking for granted, a blindness to the dynamics that form the basis of our interactions. Accordingly, we tend to think of simple trust as a continuing possibility, not just for infants, animals, and "primitive" people, but for adult humans as well.

Simple trust, like innocence, cannot be recovered if it is lost. When it is presented as an ideal, it seems a precious but always unsolicited gift that can easily be taken away. It may be true that we can never recover our innocence, but it is a tragic mistake to take simple trust as the ideal of trust and to suppose that the loss of simple trust is itself a tragedy or a disaster. The loss of simple trust, the end of that naïve transparency, is an invitation to reflection and understanding, the beginnings of wisdom. Simple trust is not "true" trust any more than a first (and equally naïve) love is "true" love. It is wonderful if we simply find ourselves trusting in circumstances that warrant our trust, but only trust in the face of doubts and concerns, trust in the world of uncertainty, is authentic trust. We may simply find ourselves trusting, but we necessarily choose and conscientiously practice authentic trust. We can also choose simple trust (plus self-deception or willful "blindness") in order to simplify our lives. But to confuse this form of self-distraction with the nature of trust itself, to confuse convenience with conviction, is to misunderstand what trust is all about.

Simple trust is not so much given as it is taken for granted; it remains unnoticed in the background of our activities. It is unquestioned not because there is nothing to question but rather because it goes unattended. We often do not realize that we have been trusting someone until our trust is betrayed, and then we are surprised both by the breach and by our having so unthinkingly trusted in the first place. But it is a mistake to take such simple trust as an ideal or as the paradigm of trust. It is desirable, this trust that is simply "there" (as a medium, as background, as "glue" or "atmosphere"), trust that can be taken for granted, trust that needs no explanation or deliberation. It is desirable as innocence is desirable, delightful in childhood and in an untroubled world, but inappropriate in this one. It is good that we try to establish trust in infants and children, giving them a core of basic trust and the beginnings of an optimistic and trusting attitude toward the world, and it is understandable that we romanticize this trust in happy children as simplicity. But for adults trust is rarely so simple. It is always plagued by doubts and fears. We can hardly be citizens of the world and trust simply (even if, as a matter of principle, we insist on "just trusting people"). But once we have given up the fantasy of simple trust, once we have faced up to life's inevitable uncertainties, then the question becomes, how can we practice authentic trust?

Giving up simple trust does not mean leaping to the opposite extreme, insisting that all trust be made explicit, scrutinized, and reinforced by sanctions or enforcement mechanisms. Once simple trust is articulated, it can be examined, qualified, and challenged. It can be turned into explicit agreements and forged into contracts. But contracts and the like are not the same as trust. Agreements and contracts may seem to *reinforce* trust, but this is misleading. It is more accurate to say that they often *replace* trust, that they explicitly spell out the possibilities of (and penalties for) betrayal, and as such represent the antithesis of simple trust. It is also a mistake to think that such agreements and contracts *precede* or *establish* trust. (There can be agreements and contracts in the complete absence of trust, typically with elaborate enforcement mechanisms).[42] But it is just as much of a mistake to conflate authentic trust with fully articulated trust as it is to conflate all trust with simple (inarticulate) trust. Our emotional life of trusting relationships is much more intricate and humanly complex than either contracts and cognitive interactive strategies or "non-cognitive security about motives" would allow.[43] Simple trust, the sort of trust that is celebrated in a well-cared-for dog, is not the paradigm to follow, but neither is the lawyer's fantasy of an "iron-clad" contract.

Blind Trust

Blind trust is not the same as simple trust. Blind trust is no longer innocent. It has been exposed to violation and betrayal. It has been presented with evidence for distrust, but it not only rejects such evidence, it denies it. Blind trust is *denial*. It is essentially self-deceptive. It can be extremely foolish (although it need not be). Amélie Rorty tells the story of a doctor who knows all the symptoms of and the prognosis for advanced uterine cancer and is unambiguously presented with the evidence that she herself has terminal cancer. She nevertheless denies her plight in order to keep practicing and helping patients for as long as possible. No one, we think, would call such self-deceptive denial "foolish."[44] Blind trust often works well, simplifying our lives when simple trust is no longer an option and helping us stick with a valuable program that more-acute reflection and thought would cause us to question.

Simple trust is just, well, simple. With simple trust, one does not even conceive of the alternative, of the possibilities of betrayal, of the grounds for distrust. With blind trust, by contrast, one denies the obvious evidence. With blind trust, one sees but refuses to see. One does not ask, or, asking, does not listen. Too often, trust as such is confused with blind trust (as loyalty is readily assimilated to blind loyalty),[45] and trust as such is taken to exclude criticism, scrutiny, and "objective" consideration of the evidence. If "objective" means simply "impartial," this is true. To trust is to be committed, and thus to be partial. But trust need be neither blind nor simple.

Authentic trust is open to evidence and the possibilities of betrayal. But blind trust is not open to evidence at all. It is closed tight to the possibility that anything could shake or betray the trust. Thus blind trust always has as one of its components an element of self-deception, or at least the will to be self-deceived. It may be that the person trusted is trustworthy and there is as yet no evidence to the contrary. To trust authentically is to be prepared to deal with such evidence. But to trust blindly is to be prepared for such evidence with a ready willingness to deny, a will to be deceived or to deceive oneself. Blind trust is rightly criticized, not because it is trust, nor even because it is "blind" (if, that is, there is nothing particularly worrisome to see). Blind trust is rightly criticized because it is willfully self-deceptive, because it refuses, or would refuse, to consider the evidence, because it engages (or is willing to engage) in complicity with untrustworthiness and even betrayal, and, accordingly, because it can be dangerous.

We can understand how easily trust can be confused with blind trust. Trust is first confused with simple trust, trust uncritical and unquestioning. When simple trust faces evidence that a person is not to be trusted, the natural reaction is denial. But even authentic trust tends to block evidence of this sort, so it begins to look as if trust is by its very nature willful, antagonistic to counterevidence, vehemently self-confirming. The differences between authentic trust and blind trust are that authentic trust is neither naïve nor self-destructive and that it "blocks" by way of resolve, commitment, and the establishment of priorities, not willful blindness. Whereas blind trust blocks evidence, authentic trust embraces it, absorbs it, and thereby neutralizes its impact as evidence for distrust. A manager who has serious doubts about the competence of her new employee but wants to "give him a chance" quite consciously resolves to tolerate his mistakes. One might say that authentic trust puts certain evidence out of play without putting it out of view, whereas blind trust simply refuses the view. There is a question of *wisdom* here, not just questions about knowledge and probabilities.

Authentic trust carries with it the knowledge of the possibility of distrust. Blind trust, by contrast, refuses to acknowledge that possibility. Trust should not be conflated with absolute, unconditional trust, but this is exactly what blind trust requires of itself. For this reason, some people consider it the "truest" trust. Military leaders and corporate bosses, in particular, mistakenly tend to praise blind trust as the only trust worth having. True trust, according to them, must be absolute. But this involves a serious misunderstanding. Trust can be prudent, measured, reflective, and conditional and still be authentic, not blind. Part of the problem with trust is that too many people refuse to consider as trust any trust that is prudent, measured, and conditional. We suggest, to the contrary, that blind trust is not really trust at all. In religious contexts, it might better be called faith, but in secular contexts, it is best identified as foolishness. To confuse such uncritical acceptance and willful denial of all possible counterevidence with trust is to misunderstand trust in the most profound way. The equation of trust with blind trust leads to the conclusion that it is never wise to trust. Trust becomes a vice instead of a virtue, a liability instead of a strength.

The primary virtue of authentic trust is that it is chosen, and it maintains that trust with considerable effort. Blind trust is also maintained with considerable effort, but instead of openness it results in narrowness and defensiveness. The exclusion of evidence is not in itself foolish or irrational. In some religious contexts, for example, believers might well insist that it is the "blindness" of the commitment, the "leap of faith," that is its greatest virtue. (Kierkegaard comes to mind. Passionate commitment is by its very nature a "leap" in the face of "objective uncertainty.") Some people would argue that in established romantic relationships and marriages, the refusal to consider the evidence is not a sign of foolishness but an exemplary feature of the love itself. The lover finds the beloved beautiful and charming, despite all "objective" evidence to the contrary. But love can be blind not only to objective foibles and flaws but also to real dangers. We may well reserve the notion of blindness, and our judgment about whether trust or love is blind, to those cases in which the refusal to acknowledge evidence is dangerous or foolish. A woman in an otherwise satisfying marriage who refuses to consider the possibility that her husband is unfaithful despite ample evidence is not necessarily blind. For her, all things considered, it may even be a wise decision.[46]

When a family member is convicted of a horrible crime, the understandable temptation is to trust kin and distrust the evidence. The refusal to abandon trust may even be considered not criminal complicity but true family loyalty. One might say that the difference between authentic trust and blind trust is to be found at that point where the evidence becomes overwhelming. So long as there remains real uncertainty, an insistence on trust despite the evidence may still be justified. But once the evidence is objectively undeniable (for example, when Theodore Kaczynski's protective brother was finally struck by the no longer deniable similarities between his brother's familiar ranting and the Unabomber's rambling prose), blind trust is no longer a virtue. From the subject's point of view, the question is not only when the evidence becomes "objectively" undeniable, but the nature and value of the relationship. Kaczynski's brother turned him in not because he had ceased to value the relationship but rather because Kaczynski had unalterably changed the relationship into one in which brotherly love was best expressed by saving his life and getting him the therapy he obviously needed.

We should note that the obstinacy and blindness to alternative evidence that are characteristic of blind trust are not uncommon with strong emotions in general. Anger, notably, has its own obstinacy and willful blindness—and this is true even before we consider a passion so extreme as "blind rage." Anger, it can be argued, sets up a kind of courtroom scenario in which the prosecution gets almost all the attention, and the outcome, as in the Red Queen's court, is more or less determined from the outset.[47] It is because of this resistance, this refusal of evidence or unbiased consideration, that anger is often called "irrational," but it is important to appreciate just how much rationality is involved in such an emotion, and similarly, how much there is in blind trust. Blind trust is not aimless. Like anger, it is intensely directed. Unlike incoherent, inconsistent thinking, emotions such as anger and blind trust are remarkably unified in their purpose, so much so that one would not be wrong in considering them, as Jean-Paul Sartre does in an early work, *strategies*.[48]

This is what is so wrong about setting up a false conflict, as Lawrence Becker does, between "cognitive strategies and non-cognitive attitudes."[49] Emotions *are* akin to strategies, even if they are inarticulate and nondeliberative. Such strategies can be articulated, and they give rise to extensive deliberation, but it is a mistake to think that by thereby being brought into the proper realm of rationality, they cease to be emotions. Blind trust (like paranoia, its polar opposite) can be impressively articulate, remarkably coherent, and on occasion convincing. But what it does—as most emotions do—is lock us into a particular perspective with well-defined boundaries, one that excludes all relevant counterevidence. Some of the most articulate strategies are expressions of the sharpest emotions—for example, in the cases of caustic resentment and moral indignation. (Perhaps we should note that these two emotions are particularly prevalent in the aftermath of a shocking betrayal of blind trust.)

Trust and Reliance: The Mechanization of Trust

We often talk about trusting inanimate objects: trusting a car to start on a cold morning, or trusting that a bridge will hold the weight of a truck. In the same way, we speak promiscuously of "loving my car" or "loving pizza," emotional attitudes different, presumably, from loving another person. But properly speaking, trust is restricted to agents, beings (usually people or human institutions) who have a choice, who make decisions, who have attitudes, beliefs, and desires, who respond to our acts and gestures with feelings, acts, and gestures of their own.

Trusting the earth beneath one's feet, on the other hand, is trust of a different order. The solidity of the earth and our trust in our own footing typically serve as metaphors for absolute reliability. (A major securities company has long advertised itself as "solid as a rock.") Anyone who has been through even a minor earthquake knows how quickly confidence can be shattered and how devastating a psychological impact can follow for weeks, months, or even years. There is good reason why philosophers talk of the "ground" of a concept or an argument, an utterly solid, unquestionable foundation. The allusion means that one can trust the solidity of the very ground we walk on—it is the unthinking presupposition of virtually every move we make—and similarly one can trust a given concept or argument. But, to put it simply, the trust we have in the earth is a trust devoid of reciprocity. The earth does not know that we depend upon it, and it doesn't care one way or the other. It does not acknowledge our trust. It does not care about our trust. It does not worry about betraying our trust. It cannot betray our trust (although in an earthquake it can severely damage our confidence).

It is important to distinguish trust from *reliance* (reliability, dependability, confidence). We often use such terms as *trust* and *reliance* interchangeably. We talk about trusting the car to start, and we talk about relying on our friends. Our intention here is not to force a pointless consistency on ordinary language but rather to map out a conceptual distinction that is of considerable importance in understanding trust. To equate trust with predictability is a mistake because we are dealing with people in dynamic, reciprocal relationships rather than with recurrent phenomena governed by (more or less) clear, lawlike regularities. Whatever we expect of the earth, it expects nothing in return, and it knows nothing of, and cares nothing about, our expectations. Camus, in both *The Stranger* and *The Myth of Sisyphus,* calls it an "indifferent universe," *la tendre indifférence du monde.* We might similarly distinguish between trust and reliance by following Camus and noting that talk about trust is relevant only when the subject is not "indifferent" in this profound sense. (Mythical personifications of the earth, such as Gaia, should not be lightly dismissed, however. Such personifications become of interest precisely because they suggest some reciprocal trusting relationship.)[50]

We talk about trusting the strength of a cross beam, or the accuracy of a barometer, or the potency of a medicine, or the dependability of twice-repaired but not yet replaced brakes in a car. In such cases, we are talking more properly about dependability, predictability, or confidence. There is no reciprocity, no agency or question of free choice involved. (The brakes do not *choose* to fail, nor do they punish us for not having them regularly inspected.) In every one of the aforementioned cases there are humans behind the scenes, designing the structure, calibrating the instrument, producing the medicine, and repairing the car. And that opens up the question of reciprocity and trust in the personal sense. But trust, properly understood, is a function of human interaction. There is trust between animals, but only insofar as they display features of interaction, communication, and reciprocity. Dogs and wolves display trusting and distrustful behavior; ants and bees do not (so far as we can discern). So trusting strange dogs may be a matter of knowledge or foolishness, but one neither trusts nor distrusts bees and other insects. One might fear them or get angry at them (for instance, after being stung or bitten), but one does not trust or distrust them. One learns to predict their behavior, no more.

To be sure, we often predict what people will do, but—and this is an essential point—trust is not the same as predictability, and without unpredictability, there is no role for trust. We make a prediction and therefore expect the mail carrier to show up at around three in the afternoon, because (and we may have no other evidence) he or she has arrived at around three in the afternoon every day for the past two years. But it would be a misunderstanding of trust and an abuse of mail carriers to treat their regular behavior as merely predictable, much less as a function of a mechanism. We trust mail carriers to show up with our mail because we understand that they are responsible human beings in a role that requires certain commitments ("Neither snow, nor rain, nor heat . . ."), [51] with a delivery strategy that makes "at around three in the afternoon" a rational plan. We are well aware that the mail carrier could decide to quit, alter the route, or abscond with the mail, but these are different from the breakdown of a mechanism. (It has been suggested that the notorious morale problems in the post office are due to the increased mechanization and expectations of efficiency there. Human beings are not mechanisms, and they resent being treated as such.) Mail carriers may be predictable, but that is because we trust them. We do not trust them just because they are predictable.

In his novel *Rum Punch,* Elmore Leonard has one sleazy character say of another, "I don't have to trust Melanie. I *know* her."[52] Here the distinction between trust and predictability is highlighted to make a point: predictability requires a high degree of probability, even a kind of (psychological) certainty. Trust requires something else: a reciprocal relationship in which questions of probability take a back seat to questions of mutual expectations, responses, and commitments. Analyses of trust in terms of predictability miss this essential aspect of trust, the element of reciprocity.[53] In what we call reliance, predictability (combined, perhaps, with a certain amount of control) is definitive. One must still make decisions about whether to rely or not rely on something, given the possibility or probability of failure or disappointment. But what is not present in reliance that is crucial in trust (and distrust) is that the person trusted has intentions and motives and makes his or her own decisions, with or without regard for the other person's decision to trust.

Trust and reliance both imply an expectation of predictability; they are also similar in the sense that our confidence always outstrips our knowledge. Trust and reliance always involve some risk; the probabilities of a favorable outcome are less than certain. And the rational warrant for trust and reliance may be seen as insufficient to justify the risk.[54] There is, in other words, an "affective leap" involved in all cases of trust and reliance, which is why trust and reliance are not merely phenomena of belief. Betting at a racetrack, with or without a detailed knowledge of the odds, does not involve trust or reliance, except at the margins—for instance, that the race is not fixed, that the horse is not sick, that the stands at the track will not collapse under the weight of enthusiastic spectators. In trust and reliance, unlike in more-detached attempts to predict the future (whatever the size of the bet), there is always an "irrational" factor, something more that does not depend only on the odds or probabilities.

An extravagant philosophical example of this "something more" is evident in the Scottish philosopher David Hume's reflections on the difficulty of justifying even the most seemingly certain predictions about the future—for instance, our trust that the sun will rise tomorrow. What Hume, in particular, did for the philosophy of trust was to point out, in a polemical way, how rationally "ungrounded" are even our most basic beliefs, those on which we have to rely to claim any knowledge whatsoever. If we cannot be confident that the future will be like the past, if we cannot rely on what we think to be the laws of nature and the inductive conclusions of our previous experience, even in terms of probabilities, then how can we claim to know anything about the world?

And yet, as Hume took away our confidence with one hand, he reinforced it with the other. Perhaps we cannot prove that the most basic assumptions of our understanding are sound, but nevertheless we can trust nature, which has endowed us with the relevant beliefs and habits. "All inferences from experience, therefore, are effects of custom, not reasoning."[55] We might not be able to prove philosophically the rationality of our confidence in reason, but outside our philosophical skepticism, what Hume calls our "sentiments" spring up "naturally" to give us that same confidence. So too, simple trust often suffices where reflection might yield a bewildering spectrum of doubts. Nevertheless, what Hume shows us quite clearly is the dubious rational support for our ordinary trust and reliance, a warning to those philosophers who would reduce trust and reliance to mere matters of belief and probabilities.

Whom Can You Trust?

We have referred to matters of trust in the natural dimension as reliance—that is, essentially, predictability. It is ultimately trust between *people* that we want to understand, and trusting people is not a matter merely of predicting their behavior. Trusting animals may be a middle-ground case, but for most of us, the question of whether or not to trust animals, or how to build trust with animals, is a secondary matter and subject to considerable debate—for example, about whether anthropomorphism (treating animals *as* people) is the best way to do this.[56] In any case, what concerns us here is creating, building, and restoring trust in human relationships and institutions, which is never a matter of mere reliance. Institutions, however, confront us with special problems.

When it comes to trust regarding such institutions as governments, markets, and corporations—the sociopolitical dimension—notions of trust and reliance become particularly problematic. Although institutions are not the same as individuals (the notion of "face-to-face" is difficult to apply to institutions, for example), institutions are human entities. They are not only human creations like bridges, skyscrapers, and theories. They are thoroughly human in the sense that they are wholly constituted, run, and moved by individual and collective human actions and decisions. The complexity arises in part because of the evasiveness of the question of responsibility. Our views are fairly straightforward when it comes to assigning responsibility to individual agents. But when a corporation "acts," it is not at all clear how its agency is to be analyzed.[57] This includes more than the assignment of credit and blame. More important, for our purposes here, are those questions about the nature of trust. Is trusting a corporation, say Motorola or Exxon, like trusting a person? Or is it more like trusting the weather or some other force of nature? To be sure, a lone individual facing a giant corporation in a credit dispute or a liability suit may well feel as if he or she is up against a faceless force of nature. But we should not put too much weight on this familiar impression. There are moments when a spouse or a teenage child also seems to be a force of nature, beyond reason and reasoning, beyond the sorts of negotiations and commitments through which trust is usually established. But we are never in any doubt (except perhaps in the extremes of mental illness) that we are dealing with a *person,* not a force of nature.

The difference between a force of nature, which can only be predicted or controlled, and a sociopolitical-financial institution, which can be considered a kind of agency, has to do with the presence of mutual consciousness. We do not merely predict and control the behavior of other people. We reason with them. We appeal to their emotions, their sympathies, their fears, their hopes and desires. On one familiar reading, corporations are thought to have only one kind of interest, their own bottom-line financial interest, but even where this cynical reading is correct, it nevertheless suggests that corporations have interests and strategies, and this leads us to consider them in human terms.

Machines and stones do not have interests and strategies. Nature does not have interests. (It is a stretch of the term, we think, to attribute "interests" to lower animals and plants, even though some conditions lead to their flourishing and others to their demise.) But if corporations have interests, even if they are only narrow economic interests, and they behave strategically, then they can be appealed to, negotiated with, depended on (or not) to fulfill their commitments. And most corporations do not think in this narrow "bottom-line" way, but rather (to varying degrees) have many interests, only some of them directly financial, and they take into account the needs and interests of a great many stakeholders, most obviously their customers and their own employees, but also the surrounding community and the larger society. What defines a corporation is not its profit margins but its sense of commitment and responsibility.

Moreover, the question of responsibility is not so amorphous as it may at first appear. A corporation (or any institution) is not a mob. Its decisions and commitments are not the actions of the herd. Every institution is also an organization, which means that it has some procedure (whether democratic, authoritarian, or by way of a small board of officers) for making decisions. Using Peter French's model of the Internal Decision Structure of an organization, we can distinguish between the opinion of someone who simply happens to be in a corporation (whether or not in a high position) and the opinion of the appropriate persons in the corporation who have the capacity to make decisions and commitments *in the name of the corporation.*[58] Even the chief executive officer of a corporation may insist on distinguishing between his or her personal opinions and his or her pronouncements as an officer of the corporation. So, in a sense, the responsibilities of a corporation—even a corporation of several hundred thousand employees and managers—are ultimately derived from the responsibilities of individual human beings.

The internal decision-making procedure of the corporation or institution might spell out the grounds for this agency, the capacity to make decisions, in a number of ways. The official pronouncements of the corporation may be nothing more than the majority view of the employees (although this approach is still relatively rare). They may, by contrast, be the dictatorial pronouncements of a single figure in his or her capacity as the director of the organization. Or, as in most corporations, the decision-making procedure might define a number of different roles by way of a hierarchy or nexus of departments, divisions, boards, and committees. What is essential, in considerations of trust, is that the corporation can and must be viewed in terms of human responsibilities. Trusting a corporation, therefore, is much more like trusting a person than relying on nature or a mechanism, whatever the complications of identifying the relevant responsible agencies. It involves human relationships, not merely prediction and control.

An unavoidable but particularly difficult concern is the motto "In God We Trust." To believe in God, most people would argue, is to trust in God. Nevertheless, it is not difficult to imagine a true believer who nevertheless thinks of God as mischievous, undependable, even malicious. The entire Hebrew Bible, for that matter, is the story of such a God and his believers. The Old Testament Jehovah is by his own admission "jealous" and "wrathful." He tests his people. The story of Abraham and Isaac is an account of one such test, in which God commands a man to kill his own son. (And this is after

God had *promised* him a son.) God countermands the sacrifice, but only after Abraham (and presumably Isaac) has been put through an excruciating ordeal. The immensity of the trust involved in this situation is such that it prompted the early existentialist philosopher Søren Kierkegaard to write a whole book about the ordeal of trust in God in the face of awful circumstances. His conclusion is perhaps the most eloquent statement we have of authentic trust. One knows and accepts the counterevidence but nevertheless chooses—passionately—to trust. Trust in God requires an unconditional trust unlike any other, a trust that may remain firm and consistent through any number of seeming betrayals. But in this sense, it is exceptional and not the paradigm.

Another text that expounds on this point is the Book of Job, in which a good man is punished repeatedly and severely in order to satisfy a wager between God and Satan. Job maintains his trust (against the advice of his friends), and God makes "makes Job whole" in the end. But the ordeal of trust as depicted in the Old Testament is extreme and quite unlike any other kind of trust. It is an ordeal repeated in modern times in the Nazi Holocaust and, on a more personal scale, in the difficult and tragic lives of many millions of faithful believers. The New Testament reaffirms this trust but suggests that trust in God and being the recipient of God's grace are not automatically correlated.[59] Trust in God is unlike any other trust in that God, perhaps, we might trust "no matter what." But with human beings and institutions, our trust must always be more circumspect and discriminating, even in our most "unconditional" commitments.

Two Virtues: Trust and Trustworthiness

Trust and the ability to identify trustworthiness are not the same thing, although trust and trustworthiness are (obviously) logically linked. Being trustworthy means, after all, being worthy of being trusted. But in recent writings on trust, trust (the act of trusting) and trustworthiness (worthiness of being trusted) are conflated and confused.[60] Trustworthiness is treated as nothing more than reliability, and thus trusting is again reduced to reliance and predictability.

Once one makes the simple distinction between the act of trusting and being trusted, it becomes clear that we are talking about a complex relationship that is by no means always symmetrical. "Trust," as a noun, is ambiguous. Accordingly, conflating trust(ing) and trustworthiness is an innocent slip, but one can see how it might well lead to confusion. For one thing, trustworthiness looks as if it has "objective" status—that is, it depends on certain facts about the person to be trusted. Trustworthiness can be demonstrated; it can be established with reasons and with evidence. Thus it reduces to a kind of reliability. This would also apply to trustworthiness backed with sanctions, where failure to fulfill one's commitment is punished. One might argue that it is not mere reliability because the interests of the person trusted are being explicitly appealed to here. But because the motive for fulfilling the commitment is the avoidance of punishment rather than respect for the commitment, one could also argue that this is not an instance of trustworthiness, merely one of prudence.

Trusting, on the other hand, might make use of such reasons and evidence, but it is more dependent on the experience and attitudes of the one who trusts than on any set of facts about the person trusted. To put the matter bluntly, one can decide to trust someone who is untrustworthy, and whom one knows to be so. One might trust a youthful criminal, just in order to teach him or her the meaning of trust, and the advantages of being trusted. And one can be perfectly trustworthy but, because of circumstances or the paranoia of everyone involved, not be trusted. No amount of factual clarification may dislodge the rigid resolve to distrust.

We have often found trust and trustworthiness confused when we are working with corporate groups and organizations. Trust is praised when it is clear that trustworthiness is what is in question. But trust as an act is treated with cautious hesitation. For instance, in one (most effective) exercise, a facilitator prompts her group to fill in the blank, "Trust is something that you _____." The usual answer is *"earn,"* clearly indicating trustworthiness. An alternative answer is *"give,"* indicating trust. The virtues of the two ways of thinking are then debated. The exercise is useful, and the shift from trustworthiness to trust is an innocent slip. But the same slip from trust to trustworthiness is not so innocent at all. It suggests a refusal to trust, or perhaps a fear of trusting.

It is a mistake, however, to push trust and trustworthiness too far apart. It seems to us clear that they are, in some nontrivial sense, two sides of the same coin. It is almost impossible not to discuss the two in tandem. Why does one trust? The answer, which seems merely trivial, is that one believes the other person to be trustworthy. And trustworthiness (perhaps like all virtues) means nothing in isolation, without trust—that is, without anyone who cares, or who is affected, or who is trusting. Trustworthiness appears to be capable of analysis in terms of reasons and evidence, but trust is fascinating precisely because it is not determined by questions of reasons and evidence. One can test someone's trustworthiness in a straightforward manner, as many sophomoric psychology experiments and television situation comedies demonstrate. Testing someone's trust, on the other hand, is a different matter. There is a real asymmetry here. One can see "how far it will go," but the connection between one's willingness to trust and the facts of the situation are tenuous at best. We might well say that trustworthiness is the "object" of trust, but between act and object there may be a significant and occasionally unbridgeable gap.[61]

We have mentioned, but have said little about, trust and trustworthiness as virtues. It is important to appreciate why they should be so considered. Trustworthiness is clearly a virtue, but trust(ing) is not obviously so. Trusting is not always a wise action. Honesty is not always wise either, but we say without pause that honesty as such is a virtue. A person who is incapable of trusting is a poor person indeed, and a society that lacks an atmosphere of trust is a society that is in many ways dysfunctional. A person who is trusting is capable of forming intimate relationships and navigating his or her way through a world in which most people are both trustworthy and trusting.

(A person living in a society where trust was nothing but gullibility and foolishness would not find trust a virtue.) To say that trust or any other suggested virtue is a virtue is not necessarily to say that it is or would be a virtue in any circumstances whatever.

One might say that trust is as much of a virtue as trustworthiness *in a trusting society*. A society that is essentially a high-trust society is capable of levels of cooperation and organization that people in low-trust societies find unimaginable. Trusting—and not only being trustworthy or dependable—is a virtue, and an inability or unwillingness to trust a vice. It is not clear that counting trust as a virtue is a way of "moralizing" trust, as Russell Hardin has charged, but it follows Aristotle in his conception of the virtues as traits of character that are conducive to a fulfilling and harmonious life in society.[62] Surely the ability and willingness to trust are among the most important of such virtues. Failing to trust someone is not merely an omission. It is *unethical* not to trust people when they are plausibly trustworthy, just as it is unethical to treat them unfairly. In fact, refusing to trust people may be more damaging to them than treating them unfairly, for the latter fails only to give them what they deserve. The former limits their capacity to act as full human beings.

Trustworthiness is a trait of character and therefore a plausible candidate for virtue, according to the standard formula. (Aristotle insists that "a virtue is a trait of character, not a passion or a faculty," or as Bernard Williams argues, "a disposition of character to choose or reject actions.")[63] One might say that one could be trustworthy just for a single occasion, but this use would seem to be a perverse application of what is usually a much more general claim. To restrict the scope of trustworthiness too much is to undermine the claim to virtue. It would be odd to say that Jones is trustworthy when it comes to taking out the garbage on Sunday when there are no other instances in which Jones can be depended on to be trustworthy. We would suspect that there is some independent reason—having little to do with trust—that prompts Jones to take out the garbage. On the other hand, we readily say that we trust Smith to show up to his appointment on time, whether or not we ever have trusted Smith, or ever will trust him, to do anything else. Thus trust(ing), unlike trustworthiness, seems episodic. Trusting can endure over time, as in a marriage or a long-term business relationship, but one might argue that trust is nevertheless made up of individual acts and choices, practices that can only be meaningful insofar as they are practiced. Thus, according to the standard formula (of virtue as a long-term disposition or state of character), it might seem that trust(ing) is not an apt candidate for virtue.

There is much that could be said about the merits of this argument, but to be brief, we reject it as embodying both a faulty conception of virtue and a too-restricted notion of trust. Aristotle's formulation blocks analysis of trust as a virtue insofar as it is a "passion," but there are passions that clearly are considered virtues. Love, for example, is a passion that certainly is often cited as a personal virtue. Although love involves episodes, it is by its very nature enduring. One might argue whether or not love is a virtue, as Plato's various spokesmen do in his *Symposium*,[64] but we should at least have some doubt about the exclusion of passion—and the emotions in general—from the list of candidates for virtue. Trust is an emotion or emotional attitude, even if it is surely not a passion in the usual sense, and, as such, we want to be careful not to exclude it from the important ethical category of the virtues. Not only individual acts but individual feelings too indicate something about a person's character, not as a "state" but as a reflection of potential. Trustworthiness is a virtue. But it is the essential part of our argument that trusting is a virtue too—that is, something that one cultivates and chooses, a practical way of living that both determines and is ultimately determined by the sorts of persons we are.

Conditional Trust

We suggested above that trust is rarely "unconditional," and even when it may be said to be properly so, it must be carefully distinguished from mere lack of discrimination or naïveté.

Before we can start to understand authentic trust, it is important that we deal in some detail with the focus, scope, and limits of trust, or what is often referred to as the "object" of trust.

The object of trust is usually taken to be some particular person or group of persons. Sometimes, as in a marriage, such a global description might make sense, but usually (and even in marriage), trust, even simple trust, is by no means all-inclusive, without conditions, boundaries, or limits. We unthinkingly trust the mail carrier to bring our mail to the front door. We are immediately suspicious if he or she suddenly starts coming around to the back door or simply walks into the house. Even naïve, simple trust has clear limits and boundaries. Because simple trust is inarticulate and devoid of distrust, it is easy enough to suppose that it is indiscriminate. But an infant's trust for his or her primary caretakers is already selective, and some dogs (dachshunds, for example) show a notoriously exclusive trust of their owners. One might have a "trusting attitude toward the world," a healthy default position, but it does not follow that trust is without limits.

This is also true concerning the range of trust within a relationship. We say that we trust so-and-so, but this usually translates into an abbreviated, context-bound description of the form "I trust so-and-so to do such-and-such." Suppose we enter into a business arrangement; I will produce shoelaces if you can supply the shoes. I trust your business acumen, your intelligence, your honesty and good sense, your knowledge of shoes. . . . Should I therefore trust you to take care of my children? This is a stupid question, but what makes it stupid? It is that trust is almost always bounded and it is usually quite specific. Even in a very specific interaction—for example, trusting the grocer to give you a fresh and untainted piece of fish at the advertised price—there are many background assumptions and hidden conditions of trust. We also trust that the grocer has not spit on the fish, has washed his or her hands, is in fact the grocer and not some imposter or alien visitor, and so on along the line of possibilities that only a philosopher, a science fiction buff, or a paranoid would devise. But the trust itself is nevertheless conditional, focused, and limited.

The scope and focus of trust is by no means self-evident. As a business partnership becomes a friendship, and the friendship becomes more involved, it may sometimes seem as if "there is nothing I wouldn't trust him or her with." But one can always find the limits, if only after they have been crossed. Marriage is of particular concern here. Suppose we spontaneously decide to get married on a starlit evening on the Love Boat. Before the boat docks in the Bahamas, the ship's captain has duly married us. I love you. Does it follow that I therefore trust you to take care of my children? This is not so stupid a question as the one directed to the shoemaker. In fact, such love-bound trust may have a much shakier foundation than trusting your children to your business associate. Business requires well-circumscribed trust, while marriage is a vast, open-ended trust. To trust the person one loves "without limits" or "unconditionally" may, however true the love, be quite irrational, for example, if there is reason to distrust his or her competence or self-control. Even love has its limits, although when we are being romantic, we like to pretend that there are no such limits.

In the English language, and in Western thought generally, there is a built-in tendency to generalize. In particular, there is a tendency to generalize trust, not to recognize its restriction in scope and focus. When we say that we "trust" someone, accordingly, we seem to imply that we trust them "in every way," and possibly "unconditionally." Thus, as Frank Sinatra sang of love, one might say "if you really trust someone, you'll trust them *all the way*." We often talk in terms of "trusting" (or "not trusting") someone, but reflection on trust seems to show that we always trust people in certain aspects, regarding the performance of certain acts and participation in well-defined practices, within certain more or less well-defined domains. Thus we may trust a spouse to be sexually faithful, but we may not trust him or her to show up on time. One might trust the dentist to take care of one's teeth but not trust him or her to take care of one's house and possessions. One might trust one's brother "implicitly" with (literally) one's very life but nevertheless not trust him to handle a shotgun.

Context and appropriateness help determine the limits of trust. We trust a business associate to remember meetings but not to remember our birthdays. We trust the leaders of a corporation to report the financial condition of the company honestly, but not to tell us about their personal lives and foibles. We frequently generalize such trust to include domains other than the one in question, but such generalization is as often evidence of thoughtlessness as it is a genuine expansion of the domain. It is always better and easier—in the absence of other information—to trust rather than to distrust, so we say simply "I trust so-and-so" rather than "I trust so-and-so to do x, y, and z," on the hopeful assumption that if someone is trustworthy regarding some actions, he or she will probably be trustworthy regarding others. Nevertheless, there are always limits, and to recognize these limits is by no means to refuse to trust. Indeed, to recognize limits is an essential part of authentic trusting.

Beyond Competence

One of the obvious conditions of trust is the competence of the person trusted. It makes no sense to trust someone to do something that he or she probably cannot do. In today's world, the obvious paradigm of trust—the one that gets appealed to in almost all of the literature—is our trust in professionals and specialists of all kinds. The world is too complicated. The tools we use are too complex to repair (much less to manufacture) ourselves. Medicine has gotten much too sophisticated and expensive to self-administer or even—when something is seriously wrong—to leave to family practitioners. The legal machinery of society has become enormously labyrinthine (largely due to the activities of the same professionals we ask to help us through that labyrinth). And so what emerges as a primary concern for trust—that is, for trustworthiness—is *competence*. We should notice, again, that marking competence as a condition for trusting too easily conflates the person trusted (whose competence is in question) and the person who trusts (whose competence resides mainly in his or her decision to trust). But competence, while obviously essential, is overplayed in discussions of trust. Competence is no more than a precondition. It is not the heart of trust.

When we call a doctor, or a plumber, or an accountant, what primarily concerns us first may be his or her competence, whether or not he or she *can do the job*. But there is a critical difference between being able to trust a person and knowing that he or she is competent. The difference has been summarized by some philosophers in terms of "having a good will"—that is, caring, as well as being competent in skills.[65] We trust the stranger who stops to help us change a tire not only to know how to change a tire, but, sadly these days, not to rob us. For new parents and babysitters, competence may be more hoped for than confidently expected (for example, the competence not to drop the baby or the competence to remember the feeding schedule and the proper formula), but it is the goodwill and good sense of the babysitter—someone who will care about the baby—that is all-important. We want to trust our doctors' knowledge and skills, but now our primary concern is whether we can trust them (or their organizations) to provide us with the best care. When doing business, we usually presume that the person or company we are addressing is competent. What we do not presume, what must both be established for us and decided by us, is whether or not to trust that person or company.

The role of competence in trust is complex. Sometimes it is the primary consideration, or, at any rate, the primary focus. We don't care whether the mechanic cares for us. We just want to get the tire fixed. Other times, notably in family relationships, competence is strictly secondary or virtually irrelevant (leaving aside the important question of interpersonal and emotional competence). But competence as such is never the sole object of trust. Even with professionals, we trust doctors not only to know what they are doing but to pay attention to what they are doing, to take into account our feelings and concerns as patients, to be not merely competent technicians but *good doctors*. Competence as such is the object of reliance, not trust. To say that trust is an interpersonal matter and not a matter of mere reliance or dependability means it is the relationship, not the ability of the person who is trusted, that is primary.

Competence is the ability to perform as expected, according to standards appropriate to the role or the task in question. To trust people involves, among other things, assessing their level of competence. It follows that an important aspect of trusting is correctly gauging this level. If a child is trusted to do a complex adult operation, failure falls not on the child but on the one who trusted the child. If an apprentice is trusted with a task that requires a master, again the blame for failure clearly accrues to the one who trusted the apprentice. (A trusting relationship can amplify or cripple competence, but this is a matter different from trusting people *because* of their competence.) Standards of competence are specific to tasks and domains, but one can distinguish different kinds of incompetence, which, accordingly, provoke quite different kinds of distrust. Trusting children or apprentices to do what they cannot (yet) do does not lead to a breach of trust. Failure must be, in an obvious sense, anticipated as a possibility. The burden is on the one who trusts, not the one who is trusted, and a negative consequence may cause disappointment but it can hardly be considered a betrayal. On the other hand, pretending to know how to do what one knows that one cannot do may well be a breach of trust. It is not the lack of competence that makes it so, but the lack of forthrightness. Here is where incompetence spills over into a violation of trust.

Trust and competence have a more complicated secondary relationship. Although competence may be a matter of reliance—that is, predictability—trusting people to inform you accurately about their competence or lack thereof is certainly a matter of trust. More complicated still is the extent to which we trust people to be honest with themselves about their level of competence. A surgeon who is getting old, a lawyer who has been fighting a drinking problem, a professor who has become a tiresome bore raise acute questions. Even if we trust them to be honest with us, we might not trust them to be honest with themselves about their loss of skills and the impairment of their judgment. Furthermore, we trust competent people to

maintain their skills, which reflects not merely on their reliability but on their character and conscientiousness. Again, we
might trust doctors to be both honest with us and honest with
themselves about their competence, but if they have not also
conscientiously kept up with the literature and the new tech-
niques of the practice, then they lack the competence we have
a right to expect from them and they have violated our trust in
a fundamental way.

When we say that trust is an emotional skill, this implies that
emotional competence is a necessary part of trust. An essential
aspect of that skill is going to be skill in judgment, in seeing the
world, oneself, and one's situation in appropriate and successful
ways. In the trades and professions, one's technical skills may be
the primary consideration, but even there it is the nature of the
relationship that is essential to trust. In marriage, in business,
and in politics, the skills involved are not easily distinguished
from the personal and interpersonal relationships of which
they are an essential part. Competence may be a key ingredient
in trustworthiness, but it is not to be separated from the emotional skills that make trusting possible.

Trust as Medium: The Most Insidious Misunderstanding

The word "trust," as a noun, seems to denote an extremely
obscure entity. We talk about relationships as constituted by
trust. We talk about trust, like love, as something one "has" for
another. We talk about trust as a general atmosphere or climate
within which people trust or tend to trust one another, as one
might talk of "ambiance" or "context." We talk about trust as
that which permeates (or fails to permeate) institutions and
organizations, as that which holds people together. One person
can give another his or her trust, and the other can "earn" it in
return. Thus trust sounds much like an entity, a *something,*
which can be exchanged, which is either present or absent,
which can be "had" or "not had," an "ingredient" in a culture
or a relationship, a "lubricant" or a "glue"—metaphors that are
hard to convert to practical use.

In sociology, understandably enough, trust is typically treated as a pervasive property of a society, community, or culture. It is an underlying sense of security, a palpable reason for confidence in an uncertain world. But when trust is metaphorically conceived of as "glue" or "a lubricant" or "atmosphere" or "a medium" or just plain "stuff," the images are all static. Trust just sits there. It is acted upon, or (as lubricant or glue) it passively facilitates or constrains action. Climate and atmosphere surround and affect, but they too are strictly impersonal and inert. Trust, on all such accounts, is inert. It simply is. And because it simply is, it can be taken for granted and, except in times of crisis, ignored.

Trust is not a medium but a human virtue, cultivated through speech, conversation, commitments, and action. It is never something "already at hand"; it is always a matter of human effort. It can and often must be conscientiously created, not simply taken for granted. Understanding trust means understanding what must be and what must not be said, avoiding those cataclysmic comments that provoke fear and suspicion. It consists of assurances, in deed as well as in word, and both the continual making and keeping of promises (trustworthiness) and the encouragement of others to make and keep their promises (trust). Trustworthiness is clearly a virtue. What is much less often recognized is that trust*ing* is a virtue—that is, trusting is a good thing to *do*. Individuals trust, and individuals collectively trust, but trust is not primarily a sociological phenomenon, nor is it a value-free cultural or sociological variable.[66] It is an essential aspect of ethics, even a matter of morality, and a matter of human interaction, choice, and responsibility. Trust is not a "given" in a lucky life but a creative part of virtually all our social practices. Trusting is a decision (or a sequence of decisions) that opens up the world for us, builds and deepens our relationships, and creates new possibilities, even "new worlds."[67]

Treating trust as a static and ultimately impersonal medium, by contrast, has one particularly vicious result, and that is contained in the familiar metaphor of *fragility*. This most insidious misunderstanding of trust turns on the idea that trust is a medium, but a fragile medium, not only in the obvious sense that it can be violated by a single untrustworthy act or statement, but in the insidious sense that it is fragile as crystal or glass is fragile. It easily breaks, and, once broken, cannot be mended. We speak of trust being "shattered" and "destroyed."

Here is the standard narrative: We start our relationships with a default attitude. True trust is "simple trust," trust that does not require our attention, trust that has as yet remained unperturbed. Or, if the situation is uncertain, we tentatively trust until trust has been established (until trustworthiness has been verified) or violated, in which case trust becomes impossible. Once established, trust can be taken for granted, or at least it is no longer an issue. Indeed, as trust becomes solidified, it is the glue that holds the relationship together. But as such, it becomes brittle. Then, perhaps suddenly, or over a long period of time punctuated by a traumatic realization, trust is betrayed. It cracks, like crystal, irreparably. And once betrayed, it is gone forever. Trust, to be true, must be solid, unspoken, unbroken, and thereby enduring. But trust is also fragile, and once broken, cannot be mended.

The danger in this narrative is the metaphor of fragility and with it the underlying metaphor of *solidity*.[68] Indeed, trust does not become an issue during much of a trusting relationship. But when trust does come into question, when it is violated or betrayed, or simply when it becomes the subject of focus, the issue is most important. Then the fragility metaphor becomes lethal. Two familiar illustrations: in the first, a man finds out that his wife of many years had been unfaithful to him before they were married. He concludes that he can no longer trust her, and so he files for divorce, ignoring all that they have been through together, all that they have built together, the identity they have jointly created. He will not be moved to forgive or forget. He is transfixed by a metaphor, by the image of irreparability. In the second, two ethnic groups, living side by side for centuries, suddenly (because of political provocation and manufactured paranoia, perhaps resurrecting some more or less historical grievance) set on each other. There are massacres, retaliations, streams of refugees. Can they get back together and ever live in harmony again? It would be awful if the answer were "no." But to assume this answer is to assume the metaphoric narrative that if trust is lost, it cannot be regained. History and personal experience tell us otherwise, but the narrative blocks our view.

Because trust is dynamic, it is much more flexible and *reasonable* than the narrative would allow. It is thus negotiable. It is never simply "solid," and it is never wholly destructible either. Taking trust for granted is always a risk, despite the truism that in a trusting relationship, trust is not an issue. But assuming that trust cannot be regained is a disaster. Trust is neither fragile nor irreparable, and the dynamics of ongoing trust and building trust dictate in turn the dynamics of restoring and renewing trust, no longer "simple" trust but a more profound, flexible, *authentic* trust.

Trust is never simply "gone," just as trust is never simply "established" once and for all. It is never finally "destroyed" so long as any semblance of a relationship—even a hostile, hating relationship—remains. Just as trust requires reinforcement, repetition, and new tests and opportunities, trust once betrayed remains open to new possibilities, new tests, and new opportunities, if only we will resolve and commit ourselves to restore that trust. And the key to restoring trust is not just earning trust but *giving* trust, even in the absence of encouraging evidence. We can resolve to ignore—not deny—even a long history of hostility and betrayal, if we keep our eyes on the long-term relationship and the possibilities for the future and refuse to dwell solely on the past. We need to trust, in other words, in the absence of trustworthiness.

If we think of trust as something that is given rather than earned, something that is created and bestowed as part of a shared social practice instead of "simply there" in a relationship or a society, trust then moves into the realm of responsibility. The loss of trust is one of those breakdowns that throws an entire practice into focus. It represents not the end of the practice but the self-conscious assessment of what it is and how it is (or is not) working. It is an opportunity for renewal as well as a danger. The real danger is not only losing trust, it is giving up on trust. The opportunity is to establish a more *authentic* trust, a trust that is indestructible as an open and mutual dedication to the relationship.

3

AUTHENTIC TRUST

The notion of *authentic trust* is borrowed from the existentialist tradition, particularly from Kierkegaard and Heidegger, although what we mean by "authenticity" can be largely separated from the theological and ontological contexts in which they presented it. Authenticity involves a keen awareness both of one's own identity and of one's relationships with others, but it also involves a deep awareness that self-identity is fluid and uncertain and that our identities change with our circumstances and our commitments to other people. Authenticity is thus a *practical* notion, and it has to do with the ways in which we together invent ourselves and reinvent our world. We feel that people who authentically trust one another live in a more vibrant and adventurous world than those who do not. People in organizations who trust one another work in a richer, more flexible, and more innovative environment than those who do not, and the organizations flourish accordingly. Politicians and people in a democracy, if they would only learn authentically to trust one another, might then forge a just and harmonious (as well as prosperous) society.

From Simple Trust to Authentic Trust

Simple trust is unreflective. Blind trust is self-deceptive. Authentic trust is both reflective and honest with itself and others. All forms of trust involve counting on other people, and, as such, they all are vulnerable to betrayal. But whereas simple and blind trust experience betrayal as earth-shattering, betrayal is neither surprising nor devastating to authentic trust. All trust involves vulnerability and risk, and nothing would count as trust if there were no possibility of betrayal. But whereas simple trust is devoid of distrust, and blind trust denies the very possibility of distrust, authentic trust is articulated in such a way that it must recognize the possibilities for betrayal and disappointment. It has taken into account the arguments for distrust, but has nevertheless resolved itself on the side of trust. Authentic trust is thus complex, and it is anything but naïve. Authentic trust is not opposed to distrust so much as it is in a continuing dialectic with it, trust and distrust defining each other in terms of the other.

All forms of trust involve relationships and interaction with other people (and are thus distinguished from reliance), but in authentic trust it is the relationship itself that is the focus of attention. In simple trust, the focus tends to be on the high degree of confidence in the person trusted and the outcome. Thus, it typically takes the form of a focused optimism. Authentic trust, by contrast, is *self*-confident rather than simply optimistic. Its focus is on one's own responsibilities in trusting. Authentic trust is trust that is well aware of the risks, dangers, and liabilities of trust, but maintains the self-confidence to trust nevertheless.

Making distinctions among simple, blind, and authentic

trust is important as a way of emphasizing the special virtues of authenticity as opposed to the naïveté and self-deceptive obstinacy that are often identified and celebrated as trust. In drawing these distinctions, we are not delineating different kinds of trust. Formulating such typologies has become a favorite sport of commentators; consider Bernard Barber's classic distinctions among technical or professional competence, fiduciary responsibility, and social (moral) trust writ large, Patrick Murphy and Gregory Gundlach's five-part distinction among "calculative, verifiable, reciprocal, earned, and blind" trust, and other such distinctions as in Shapiro, Sheppard, and Cheraskin's three-part division of "deterrence-based, knowledge-based, and identification-based trust."[69] We want to cast a skeptical eye on all such sets of distinctions, not only because they tend to bureaucratize complex organic phenomena but also because they tend to ignore the dramatic interplay between intelligence and strategy, affect and cognition, and vulnerability and risk. Rather, while allowing a certain space for simple trust—for example, among small children and within families—our whole project is dedicated to rejecting most so-called types of trust *as not being trust at all.*

Competence is almost always an ingredient in trust, but competence by itself is different from trust. Trust can be earned, but to link trust so closely to trustworthiness, knowledge, and verification is to remove all significance from the act of trusting. Calculative, deterrent, and strategic trust are fraudulent versions of trust with an eye to one's own advantage, and so not really *trust* at all. And blind trust belongs to a different realm of phenomena altogether; it is a phenomenon of self-deception.

Authentic trust is constituted as much by doubt and uncertainty as by confidence and optimism. This is a thesis that has often been argued with respect to religious faith. One might compare Augustine, Kierkegaard, and Dostoyevsky on faith. All three experienced intense periods of doubt and despair, but all three came to see this as not antithetical to faith but essential to it. Faith, in other words, is not "simple"; it is a matter of authenticity. Authentic trust, like true love and genuine faith, is possible only in the light of a *breakdown* of trust (or love, or faith). One cannot authentically trust unless one has experienced, if only vicariously or in imagination, disappointment, loss, or betrayal. What makes simple faith simple is that it has had no such experience. What makes blind faith blind is that it refuses to associate *this* instance of trust with any previous experiences of disappointment, loss, or betrayal. ("My boss is different. She would never betray her employees." "But Sam isn't like all the others. I trust him completely!") One need not actually suffer from a breakdown in *this* particular relationship in order for trust to be authentic. The very thought of losing or disappointing one's beloved may spur true love. The mere thought of betrayal is often essential to authentic trust.

Authentic trust, as opposed to simple and blind trust, does not exclude or deny distrust, but rather accepts it and goes on to transcend it in action. One might even say that authentic trust embraces distrust and involves the willful overcoming of it, not just as a matter of attitude but as a matter of practical interaction. Authentic trust differs from simple and blind trust in its willingness—indeed, in the necessity—to confront distrust. Practically, one does this by confronting the other person. So much of the literature on trust focuses its attention on trust as an attitude or as a social medium that the most important features of trust are ignored—conversation, communication, *negotiation*. Even in the most difficult cases of building trust, between age-old ethnic enemies or longtime warring factions, the key ingredient isn't some magical transformation of attitude so much as it is the possibly drawn-out tedium of bringing the sides together and making some mutual commitments, perhaps starting with small and seemingly insignificant promises. In Vietnam, in Korea, in Palestine, in Bosnia, in Kosovo, the narrative in any attempt at reconciliation has always been the articulation of distrust, the airing of grievances and aspirations, the swapping of accusations and threats, the slow coming together of mutual acknowledgment and, eventually, shared identity and mutual respect. (Trust does not require agreement. It requires commitment and authenticity. Diplomats are fond of saying, "as long as they keep talking . . ." —not because talk necessarily prevents bloodshed but because as long as there is conversation, there is hope for trust.

The complex interactions that lead to authentic trust suggest what is necessary to move from simple trust to authentic trust. They are, in a few words, self-scrutiny, caring about the long-term relationship and not just the outcome, negotiation and mutual understanding, a willingness to make and stand by one's own commitments, a keen awareness of the risks and liabilities, and the recognition that taking on these risks and liabilities is above all one's own responsibility.

Authentic Trust

One of the issues most often discussed by philosophers interested in trust is the weight and rationality of evidence justifying trust—that is, the evidence for the trusted person's trustworthiness. We, by contrast, consider the weight of the evidence at best a secondary concern, because *trusting changes both the person trusted and the person who trusts.* Trusting is a choice, a decision, and authentic trusting takes into primary account the way the relationship will change as the result of that choice. For instance, a father trusts his young son to carry out a task for the first time. There is no evidence that the son is competent or mature enough to do so, but by being trusted, he comes to acquire both competence and maturity. And the relationship between father and son obviously changes. The father comes to respect his son, which is different from simply loving him or having affection for him. The son gains a modicum of independence from his father, but, more important, he comes to understand his own desire to please his father, to solidify the relationship on a new basis. Similarly, consider a boss trusting a new employee to take charge of a project. The boss has only a general sense of the employee's background and competence, but in giving the employee the assignment, the boss establishes a new relationship with the employee, and the employee wants to do the job well both for the sake of his or her own sense of self-worth and to please the boss.

Thus we should be careful about the "evidentiary" approach to trust. We understand why such an approach can be attractive, not only for philosophers but for anyone in charge who must decide whom to trust. The evidentiary approach promises to make trust more rational. Unlike simple trust, it demands *reasons* for trusting. Unlike blind trust, it insists on an open, scientific mind, considering all the evidence. But trust is always more than evidentiary. It always outstrips the evidence that would rationally justify it. This does not mean that trust is always "irrational." Rationality is not only found in the accumulation of evidence; it is also identified in terms of *what one really cares about*.[70] Trusting is also rational because it is a way of creating, maintaining, deepening, and restoring relationships. It is not the weight of the evidence that makes trust rational or irrational. It is the desirability of the end, the relationship—and in this case at least, the end justifies the means.

Authentic trust develops not from a scientific "wait and see" attitude but through engagement with the other person or people. People do not develop trust by forming affective attitudes or beliefs *about* another person. They develop trust through interaction and conversation, in relationships *with* each other. Here, as so often, the philosophical bias is in favor of the formation of attitudes and beliefs *in one mind* ("the subject") *about* another ("the object"), but trust is to be found in interactions and relationships, not in an isolated mental attitude.

Authentic trust is by its nature articulated trust, trust that is "spelled out." As such, it becomes an *issue*. This has a double significance. For both parties, becoming aware of their obligations and responsibilities intensifies their sense of mutual identity and the significance of the relationship for each of them. (This need not always work in favor of trust, we should note. Becoming aware of one's obligations and responsibilities can also breed resentment.) But just as important, making trust an issue allows it to be talked about and negotiated. (In simple trust, by contrast, an invitation to talk about trust is usually treated with dismissal: "Oh, of course I trust you. There's nothing to talk about." This is also true of cordial hypocrisy.)

In business contexts, trust is almost always an issue. Whether it is the quality of the product or the promptness of the delivery, whether it is attentiveness to the customer or the loyalty of the employee, whether it is respect for the importance of confidential information or the need for a joint strategy, the issue is trust, which will be articulated and negotiated, whether or not in the form of an explicit verbal agreement or a written contract. This does not mean that trust in business is always authentic trust. Indeed, authentic trust is all too rare, insofar as traditional business attitudes virtually dictate the focus on the bottom line, the outcome of the transaction. But insofar as a business takes seriously the *relationship* aspect of its operations, building relationships with customers, employees, suppliers, and the surrounding community, trust really does become the focal issue, and such a business is far more likely to succeed over the long run.

Authenticity also requires a kind of self-scrutiny that businesspeople often reject. In the name of loyalty to the company, in the name of the fixed definition of one's role or position ("that's not my job"), in the name of the financial ("bean-counting") aspects of the business, people all too often take themselves—that is, their *selves*—and the identity of the company for granted. But in the current business world, it should be obvious that the identities of companies, the identities of whole industries, and accordingly the identities of all the people who work in those companies and industries, are in constant transition. Many of the major industries in the world today did not exist a few years or decades ago, and most of the companies that have been in business over that time have radically changed their identities accordingly. (Think GE [General Electric], AT&T ["Ma Bell"], NCR [National Cash Register], IBM [International Business Machines].)

Simple trust, the trust that is typically found in family relationships, can become authentic. It is often forced to become so in the face of crisis and the breakdown of family relationships. Families that have suffered through the tragedies of alcoholism and drug addiction, or families that have faced severe financial hardship and a traumatic end to an accustomed way of living, discover that the bonds that for many years had remained merely implicit and taken for granted now must be brought into the open, made into issues, and negotiated—often with great emotional pain. Basic trust can thus be reconstituted, no longer as simple or blind but as truly authentic. A family that comes successfully through such an ordeal may well have scars. (Authentic trust is by no means the most pleasant form of trust.) But there is a serenity that comes with resolution, and this is something quite different from the false sense of well-being that comes from ignorance and naïveté or the anything-but-serene, suppressed angst associated with self-deception and blind trust.

Authentic trust is marked by this self-confidence; one becomes both sure of oneself and confident of one's capacity to deal with the outcome, whatever that may be. Authentic trust, unlike blind and simple trust, has much more to do with self-awareness—knowing who one is and what one is all about—than with simple prediction and reliance. Families that have emerged from the transition to authenticity have come to terms with themselves in a way (often the only way) that allows them continue as a family, and, as many such families have attested, they are thereby stronger and more intimate than ever before.

One need not, however, suffer such trauma in order for trust to become authentic. At the heart of authentic trust is the idea of self-conscious commitment. It is what makes trust an issue and raises the basic questions of self-identity and relationships. Although there are implicit and tacit commitments, what is most significant about commitments is that they necessarily involve reciprocity and communication. Although commitments can be indicated without words (a nod of the head will sometimes do), they require communication and mutual understanding.

A commitment is not merely a set of expectations. If I make a commitment to deliver the shipment to you by Friday, you can expect the shipment by Friday. But you might expect the shipment by Friday without any commitment on my part (for example, because I am always in a hurry to unload my inventory as quickly as possible), or I may fulfill your expectations because I happen to be in the mood to do so (perhaps I look forward with curiosity to seeing the look of delight on your face). A commitment is (more or less) explicit and mutually understood. Trusting people without their knowing, like loving people without their knowing, is a secondary phenomenon. Trust, like love, is paradigmatically a matter of relationship, not mere attitude.

It is because trust is predominantly interactive that it necessarily opens up the possibility of betrayal. Betrayal violates the mutual understanding. (Where there is only a misunderstanding, the accusation of betrayal is usually dismissed.) But not all of the features and conditions of authentic trust must be articulated. It is clearly impossible to spell out all the implicit conditions and possibilities in any interaction (as contract lawyers know all too well). But the focal points of the trust, its various vulnerabilities and liabilities as well as the expectations and conditions for satisfaction, must to some extent be a matter of both individual and mutual awareness.

Authentic trust is emphatically not "strategic," although it is almost always optimal in its long-term results. This could be construed as a paradox: we trust without regard for our long-term advantage in order to gain a long-term advantage.[71] But in our discussion of trust and trustworthiness as virtues, we noted that all virtues have this paradoxical form: their goal or purpose is not self-interested even though their function and outcome is much more often than not in the greater interest of one person (or both). A person is generous because she is moved by the plight of another, or because she feels an obligation to help out, but if she thinks too much (what philosopher Bernard Williams calls "one thought too many") about how this will enhance her reputation or how this will make the recipient grateful and indebted, it is no longer generosity. We trust because it is right to trust, not because we are simply pursuing our own advantage. Nevertheless, there is no way better to secure our own advantage than through trust, and trust has virtues and advantages that are distinct from any calculation of risks and probabilities. Insofar as trust is merely a calculation of risks and probable advantages, it is not authentic trust. If we wanted to play the typology game, perhaps we could call this "prudential trust." It is the conception of trust that emerges out of game theory, rational choice theory, and the like.[72] But authentic trust is not primarily concerned with advantages, even though the large-scale expectation of long-term and general mutual advantage may be an important ingredient in its motivation and justification. To put an end to the apparent paradox: authentic trust is *primarily concerned with the integrity of relationships,* not with personal advantage, whether in the short or in the long term. Nevertheless, trust is almost always a precondition for personal advantage, both in the short and in the long term, growing out of the relationship.

In business, questions about the integrity of relationships—even if they are narrowly construed and relatively short-term relationships—are of central importance. Consider a nonbasic form of security, the sort of security that bears that name, "security" —an ambiguous word. A security is both property deposited as a pledge, something that secures, and an investment, a financial instrument, a share of stock or a bond, for example. No matter how naïve the investor, the presumption is that a good deal of consideration and attention has gone into the investment, and trust is involved on many levels. Novices in the stock market may have simple or even blind trust in their brokers, but experienced investors know better. That they remain wary does not mean that they trust less, however. They trust more wisely. They recognize the need to combine trust with information and vigilance. Thus it is assumed: investors have articulate, authentic trust. Business is shot through with this assumption, from caveat emptor to the presumption of understanding and the absence of coercion that underlies every business contract. Again, the contract must be seen as secondary, trust as primary. Edward Deming had it right—and it is not incidental that he taught it most successfully to the Japanese: you don't just do business. You build relationships. In other words, you develop trust.

The weighing of trust and distrust is so essential to trust in business—and to authentic trust—that the idea that trust and distrust are mutually exclusive, in a business context, makes no sense. Simple trust is out of place in business (which is why, mistakenly, "hard-headed" businesspeople sometimes think that trust is inappropriate as well). Blind trust is downright foolish. As the old cliché would have it, "business is business," which means that vigilance is always in order. Every business deal involves risk, and so every business deal involves some form of (usually limited) vulnerability. What makes it "business" is (more or less) wise choice in trusting and distrusting, but this can only be authentic trust, trust that has already transcended any simple childish or what George Santayana called "animal" faith.[73] And authentic trust involves an awareness of risks and vulnerabilities and requires a keen assessment (not "calculation") of the person, the relationship, the situation, the stakes, and, most important, the unknown future that will be opened up by trust. It is this last uncertainty that makes authentic trust always a matter of commitment and never just calculation.

Finally, authentic trust involves *choice*. Consider a woman confronted with evidence of her husband's possible sexual infidelity. In such situations, it is not possible simply to assume trust. One must straightforwardly *decide* the matter. She must decide, in the face of the evidence, whether or not she will continue to trust her husband, with all that implies. That means, for example, that she will not pursue the "inquiry," will not go on asking probing questions, will not allow herself to look at him or inspect his activities with unusual scrutiny. It also means that she will exercise herself in possibly more difficult psychological maneuvers—for instance, not allowing herself to be repulsed or otherwise negatively affected by his touch, nor allow herself to be randomly ironic in other matters or in her use of metaphors with romantic, sexual, or fidelity-bound considerations. It may mean a selective choice of friends or, at any rate, careful selection of what she will listen to or not listen to or allow them to say or not to say. To be sure, much of this display is acting *as if* she still trusts her husband, but it is through such *as if* behavior that trust is authenticated. On the other hand, it is also by means of such *as if* behavior that the betrayal can be confirmed and confronted.

Or consider a business partner who suspects that one of his associates may be misusing project funds to further interests of his own. He may simply make an accusation, thus seriously altering the relationship and most likely ending the partnership. Or he may keep quiet but resolve to watch his partner carefully and never to trust him again, thus rendering the partnership all but inoperative. Or he might let on that he has "concerns," but subtly bypass any accusation, inviting, clearly but tacitly, some sort of confirmation of trust. But here again the appearance of paradox comes into play. He acts *as if* he trusts his associate in order to see if he can trust the associate, or, to put it more pointedly, he acts as if he trusts the associate precisely because he does not trust him and is in effect setting a trap in which the betrayal will be revealed. But here again, the sharp division between trust and distrust is derived from the all–or–nothing model of simple trust. It is inappropriate for authentic trust. Authentic trust, unlike simple trust, is an ongoing, delicate dance of trust and distrust, the tests and trials of commitment, the careful scrutiny and reassessment of the relationship.

This existentialist model of authentic trust as a series of decisions has the distinct advantage of putting trust back in our hands, making it less mysterious, less an "it" that is there or not there and more a part of both the continuing relationships we have with other people and the way we define our identity with and through those others. The virtue of putting trust (and distrust) back in our own hands is also its liability, however, for it now begins to sound as if we could decide to trust *at will*. We all know how hard, if not impossible, this can be, particularly after a betrayal or in the face of suspicious and undeniable evidence. We do not and cannot simply "choose" to trust or not to trust, in part because we cannot always choose our circumstances, or the people with whom we become involved, or the history of that involvement. Nor can we simply choose our own psychology, our own needs and reactions, our habits, perceptions, and attitudes. We seem to be stuck in our moods and our views of the world (optimism and pessimism, for example), and there is, apparently, little we can do to alter them. (So, too, Fukuyama writes as if cultures are "stuck" with their low-trust/high-trust characters, and there is nothing that they can do to change those attributes.) That is why we must ultimately come to understand trust in terms of coming to grips with our emotions and moods. Authentic trust is ultimately a skill and, in particular, an emotional skill.

Trust as Emotion

We have suggested that trust is a matter of emotion, comparing it to love. This is not to say that trust consists of distinctive "feelings" —although feelings such as affection, anxiety, confidence, hope, relief, and gratitude are familiar aspects of the experience of trusting someone. (Love, too, is not so much a distinctive feeling as it is an enormous range of sensitivities, dispositions, practices, and commitments.) Distrust, we might add, is also accompanied by a rich range of feelings, notably anxiety, resentment, and fear. Indeed, our negative emotional repertoire tends to be much more fine-grained and expansive than our rather impoverished set of positive emotions. There is no greater trauma than trust betrayed except, perhaps, love betrayed, for love typically, perhaps necessarily, involves the most profound trust and so gives rise to the most violent reactions when betrayed. It is not just a cliché of the romantic genre that love and hatred are kindred emotions, and that betrayed love and vengeance go hand in hand. This is the logic of emotions, and the quiet calm of trust finds itself locked in the matrix of such violent passions.

One might question whether trust should be counted as an actual emotion. Unlike anger, fear, or obsessive love, trust displays none of the violence of the soul, the explosiveness, that we associate with the emotions. Although the betrayal of trust certainly breeds such emotions, trust itself quietly continues, silently stretching over years or decades. But this description reflects a prejudice about emotion (or "passion") that goes back to ancient times, the notion that all emotion is violent, even "mad," the idea that emotions are interruptions or intrusions into rational life rather than the very foundations of life.

Not all emotions are violent, explosive, overwhelming, or intrusive. Trust, in particular, is most evident in its modesty, in its quiet expression, in its congeniality, in its subtle pervasiveness. Without trust, we would all quite rightly be "mad," but this does not mean that trust is not an emotion.

Trust is not like anger or jealousy (although the clear identity of jealousy as an emotion indicates that distrust, at least, has close emotional kin). Anger and jealousy are both reliably specific emotions, although both have their variations and applications, and they both can be readily identified, not merely associated, with quite specific "feelings" (although these feelings may be much more cognitively and socially complex than the usual "feeling angry" talk would suggest). In addition, many of the feelings provoked or evoked by anger are not themselves "feelings of anger" (for example, the desire for revenge, or a sense of indignation). Trust, on the other hand, has no such specific feelings, nor does it seem to be the sort of thing that is usually called an "emotion." We think of emotions as noisy, as commotions, and our metaphors for emotional expression often reflect a certain violence—for instance, "he blew his top" means he got very angry. But emotions need not always be so noisy. Two people can quietly love one another for decades, and David Hume talks at length about the "calm" (as opposed to "violent") passions and about the "moral sentiments" with which trust might be considered.[74]

One might argue that trust is more steadfast than many emotions, in that, unlike fits of anger or pangs of jealousy, for example, it endures through time. But so, too, can love; even emotions such as anger, jealousy, grief, sadness, resentment, and envy can also be abiding, not easily localized in time in our experience. (Betrayal, by contrast, can often be pinpointed to the minute.) In this sense we might better think of trust and all such steadfast emotions as what Heidegger called a "mood," a way of "being tuned" into the world.[75] Thus, in a deeper sense, we might consider trust as an emotion not because it is merely psychological or in some misleading sense "inner" but because it is a profound way of defining our relation to the world.

Trust and trustworthiness both depend on emotional attitudes, but different ones. Trust involves feelings of mutuality, dependency, and confidence. It is not merely incidental that trusting someone is often described in terms of feelings. Trustworthiness, on the other hand, is not so plausibly described as a feeling. Nevertheless, it typically involves feelings of respect, of obligation and duty, of affection and responsibility. Putting these together, we might say that both authentic trust and authentic trustworthiness involve feelings derived from and directed to a relationship, and in this (again) they are a lot like love. The emotions of the lover are not the same as the emotions of the beloved; with good reason, attention has long been focused (since Plato at least) on the feelings of the lover. So, too, our concern here is with the emotions and moods of the person who trusts rather than the person trusted. As in love, however, the ideal (and not at all uncommon) situation is the one in which all of this is mutual, and each partner in the relationship is both lover and beloved, the one who trusts and the one who is trusted.

One problem in talking about emotions in the realm of trust and interpersonal ethics in general is the traditional primitivization of emotions; emotions are taken to be simple bodily feelings or sensations or just dumb (unthinking, noncognitive) attitudes. This too easily leads to the conclusion that trust, insofar as it is an emotional phenomenon, has nothing to do with knowledge and understanding; it is just intuition and "raw feeling." And this leads us back to simple trust, trust unarticulated, unexamined, accepted simply at face value. But although trust necessarily involves emotions, it is also a matter of knowledge, of recognition, even of planning and strategy. Trust is not a matter of mere cognition—that is, of the recognition of the contingencies of the situation and the relationship and its possibilities. Trust also means *caring* about them. *Care* is perhaps the most essential ingredient of authentic trust, not only care about the immediate outcome but care about the relationship. Without caring, what is called trust is no more than prediction and reliance.

Emotions themselves are now generally understood as "cognitive" phenomena; they are partly learned (as well as partly biological responses), involve not only comprehension but evaluation of circumstances, and are themselves a mode of understanding. Love, for example, is keenly aware of the beloved, not just his or her features, details, history, and so forth, but also of his or her importance in the lover's life. Love does not merely find but also bestows and appraises the value and virtues of the beloved.[76] Love *makes* the beloved beloved. Authentic trust is much like this, and its most important single consequence is that it bestows, as well as appraises, the other person's virtue. In other words, trusting people—just like loving them—not only appreciates and depends on the other people. It *changes* them, and usually for the better.

To say that trust is an emotional phenomenon and a way of "tuning into" the world is to say that such "tuning" is something we can cultivate and, within certain limitations, control. Such talk makes no sense if we remain under the impression that emotions are nothing but physiological phenomena or merely physical feelings, There is a long-standing belief that our emotions just "happen," that they are beyond the realm of choice and therefore outside the realm of responsibility. This is wrong on several counts. First, we can certainly be held responsible for controlling our emotions, or at least for controlling our expressions of emotion. Moreover, it can be argued that we should take a great deal of responsibility for our emotions because we often choose the situations in which we find ourselves. We put ourselves into situations in which it is likely that one or another emotion will be evoked, and we often choose the people with whom we spend time. In short, we often decide the causes of our emotions. Furthermore, we can resolve to change our emotions or moods—for example, by talking to the other person. Emotions can seem like traps if we spend our time brooding on them. But consider the example of anger: expressing or simply reporting our anger to the person at whom we are angry will almost certainly initiate some dialogue, even if only out of indifference or surprise, which will in turn alter the emotion—perhaps exacerbating it rather than resolving it, but in any case putting it "on the table" to be dealt with, together.

What we would like to suggest is that emotions in general and authentic trust in particular are both chosen and a person's responsibility—or people's collective responsibility.[77] First, and most important to our concerns here, emotions can be cultivated. Trust can be cultivated. It can be initiated, generated, and repaired. We cannot simply decide to trust, or to feel virtually any other emotion. We can rarely simply choose to do anything; choices require implementation and instrumentality. In one sense, the choice is only the first step. (In a more ordinary sense, the choice is the entire course of events that begins with the initial resolution.) But our claim is that, in an important sense, we choose to fall in love, to get angry, to be jealous, to trust. (Distrust, too, is a choice.) The evidence in favor of trusting may be overwhelming, in which case the choice may be so obvious that it does not seem like a choice at all. But often the evidence is only partial, and there is at least a whiff of suspicion. That is when the element of choice becomes most obvious and the need for discussion most imperative.

One might argue that we are not responsible for our beliefs, and therefore we cannot be responsible for the emotions that follow from those beliefs.[78] But we are responsible for our beliefs, although we do not choose a belief as we might choose to entertain a thought. Even if we simply absorbed our beliefs as we were growing up (consider, for example, racist beliefs), we are responsible for examining them, criticizing them, and cultivating alternative beliefs when it becomes evident that our old beliefs are somehow wrong.[79] Authentic trust consists, to at least some extent, in deciding what to believe, and, more importantly, resolving to create the circumstances in which these beliefs will be justified.

It makes an enormous difference whether we view trust as simply a feeling that follows from certain rudimentary beliefs about a person's reliability, or rather think of trust as a process of which we are an essential part, and for which we bear responsibility, which we can create and maintain as well as destroy. Rather than thinking of emotions as mere feelings or physiological phenomena—things that happen to us—we would be better off thinking about emotions as *investments*.

This might strike some as an overly economic approach to areas as personal as trust and the emotions. On the contrary, however, the notion of investment is itself not primarily economic but emotional, having to do with our sense of being in the world and our caring about other people and our relationships with them.[80] Trust, in particular, is a personal investment. It involves feelings, to be sure, but these feelings are a response to (or, more accurately, accompany our responses to) threats and reassurances regarding our investments. But an investment is something we *make*. We take responsibility for our investments. One invests not only in a preferred outcome but in a relationship, and cares personally about its success. We all have an investment in our "selves" —that is, not only our very beings but the way we think of ourselves and the way others think of us. This dimension of our being is what we often call our "integrity," and it is closely related to the authenticity that is central to authentic trust. Authentic trust is an emotional phenomenon because it is not merely a way of understanding and predicting the world, but a way of investing in it, of looking forward to a future that the investment itself helps make possible.

Trust as Mood

What we have said here about emotions can readily be applied to the broader concept of *mood*. Heidegger is talking about mood when he suggests that we are fundamentally "tuned" to the world in distinctive caring ways. The difference between an emotion and a mood is the specificity of focus. An emotion is directed at a more or less specific object, often another person or another person's behavior. A mood, by contrast, encompasses the world. One may become depressed not just about this event or that tragedy but "about everything," or more accurately, about whatever specific object happens to come along. So, too, in an ecstatic mood, one finds oneself overjoyed by whatever or whoever should happen along. One is usually angry (as an emotion) at some particular person or group of persons, but one can also be in an angry mood, in which case almost anything is capable of triggering anger. A mood can define a person's social character ("grumpy," "enthusiastic," "morbid," "pious") as well as his or her way of what Heidegger calls Being-in-the-World.

Love is typically directed toward a particular person, the beloved. But Erich Fromm writes at length about the primary importance of being "a loving person."[81] Although trust is usually directed at a particular person, group of persons, institution, or organization, one can be in a trusting mood or, more generally, be a trusting person. Here what we have said about the amenability of emotions to cultivation and change becomes particularly important for moods. A mood is not just something that happens to us, like a storm passing overhead (or through the head, as in many popular "internal weather" metaphors). We often think of moods, even more than emotions, in a primitive way. Psychoneurologists have accumulated impressive knowledge about the chemical "causes" of depression, for instance, but their invaluable discoveries have often been extended into the absurd thesis that depression—and every other emotion and mood—is *nothing but* brain chemistry and its consequences.

Less scientifically, people attribute their moods to *what has happened to them*. Their thinking about moods is thus backward-looking, and they are mainly concerned with "getting out of" the mood in question. But just as it is important—practically, even more than theoretically—to think of emotions not as happenings, with ourselves as their victims, but rather as a kind of "doing" for which we are responsible, moods, too, should be viewed as future-oriented ways of engaging with the world. We should concern ourselves not with what has happened but with *what is to be done*. We should attempt not to get out of the mood but to *realize* it. Moods, like emotions, are not "inner occurrences" but dynamic orientations toward the world and other people.

We have moods because we care. But caring can take many forms, from despair to love, and the moods we have determine to a large extent the range of our actions (and our feelings as well). Thus cultivating moods, and in particular cultivating moods conducive to trust, is an important part of any human relationship, from the intimacies of marriage to the complexities of a giant corporation. Loving does not automatically lead to trusting (and neither does being loved), but clearly the intimacy of love is not only conducive to but spurs the need to trust as well. Conversely, suspicion and distrust undermine love.

One or both partners in an unhappy marriage may adopt a mood of resignation, probably as protection against further disappointment. In so doing, such people must refrain from taking any assertive action, and close off the possibilities of negotiation and mutual understanding that might lead to an improved relationship. In the face of an impending catastrophe, one may fall into despair, which shuts down all hope (and thus the intelligibility of any preventive action). In a marriage, the logic of the self-fulfilling prophecy is almost always operative. One thinks his or her mood is nothing but a response to what has happened, but it is the mood that is shaping the future and possibly bringing about precisely the situation that supposedly caused the mood in the first place. Jealousy is a rich example that has a good deal to do with trust and distrust. How many times has a beloved been driven off by a lover's jealous mood, in which distrust has created the distance that the jealousy thinks it merely discovered?

In a corporation or any complex organization, moods are primary determinants of dedication, efficiency, and success. Corporate moods are often summarized misleadingly as "morale," but this is a simpleminded term that tends to reduce to two simpleminded categories, "good morale" and "bad morale." But within the scope of bad morale, there are many different moods. There is resignation ("Nothing is going to improve this situation, and there is nothing I can do to change it"). There is despair ("Nothing can prevent this total calamity. We might as well just let it happen"). There is straightforward distrust ("I don't believe what they told me, so I'm certainly not going to put my heart into it"). There is full-scale cynicism ("Nothing ever changes, and nothing ever gets better, so it is silly even to try"). There is confusion ("I don't know what's going on here and I don't know whom to ask, and I can't afford to let anyone know that I don't know what I'm doing"). And there is panic ("I'll never be able to do this!").

We are all painfully familiar with bureaucratic moods, which are often conflated with "policy." Such moods dictate a retreat from personal responsibility and judgment, typically in the name of following rules. There are *faux heroic* moods, in which everyone pretends an exaggerated self-confidence that blocks both innovation and communication and betrays a fatal lack of confidence. There are *opportunist* and *survivor* moods, in which an "every-man-for-himself" mentality rules as a perverse kind of collective conformity.[82] And there is that often celebrated but usually misunderstood *competitive* mood, which is thought to be the engine of free enterprise but within an organization more often leads to mutual distrust and even mutual sabotage, much to the disadvantage of the organization as a whole.

The distinctions among these different bad moods are to a large extent due to different assessments of the situation, but they also point to different cooperative (or uncooperative) relationships. To call the pervasiveness of distinctive bad moods "bad morale" is merely to dismiss it as a sad fact of corporate life. To recognize the specific moods as what they are, self-chosen and culturally endorsed ways of being in the organization and the world, is to open up the way to change them.

The most devastating of all bad moods is the mood of resentment. Resentment is the most devastating because it is directed not at a situation but rather directly at other people (one's boss, one's colleagues, the organization in general). Resentment is even worse than distrust (and it inevitably leads to distrust) because it also tends to be vengeful. Employees who distrust the management may not believe what they are told and consequently may not be willing to work hard, but the employee who resents the management also wants to "get even." Corporate sabotage is typically a product of resentment, as are thousands of lawsuits and millions of disgruntled customers. Nietzsche writes at considerable length about the damage done by resentment, particularly to those who harbor the resentment themselves. "His soul squints," he writes of the resentful man who allows his own sense of importance and wounded merit to fester inside him until he is poisoned by it and incapable of creative or constructive action. To dismiss as "bad morale" what may well be a culture of resentment is to leave oneself open to almost inevitable catastrophe.

All of these "bad morale" moods can be contrasted with the trusting mood that allows companies and the people who work for them to flourish. To trust is to be open and look to the future, even in the face of the same challenges and catastrophes that in other contexts give rise to such bad moods as resignation, confusion, and despair. Instead of resignation or despair, there is engagement and commitment ("What can I do?"). In place of confusion, there is the clear conviction that those in charge know what is going on, that they can be engaged in productive conversation, and that one can unhesitantly admit that one needs advice or direction. Whereas resentment sulks and stews and plots revenge, trust opens up, and (with others) maps out the future. Obstacles are viewed as challenges, and challenges are opportunities. In place of confusion there is a sense of resolution ("I am going to take action right now"), and in place of panic there is acceptance and serenity ("I know that the future is uncertain, but I am grateful for the opportunity to play my role in it").

It is only in such contexts that overused expressions such as "team spirit," "empowerment," and the seemingly archaic "loyalty" really mean something. It is true that the "good old days" of a job for life and the parental company ("Ma Bell," Tom Watson's IBM "family") are gone. But what has taken their place is a new and exciting set of possibilities, in which comfort must be replaced with self-confidence, and trust—not just the simple trust of continuing familiarity, but authentic trust—becomes utterly necessary.

How do we cultivate good moods, the moods of trust, and how do we get rid of the bad moods, the moods that destroy relationships and organizations? Here the idea that emotions and moods are "cognitive" becomes all-important. We transform a mood not by identifying the cause of the mood but rather by identifying the assessments about the future that make up the mood. Because most of these assessments are not so much about the situation as about the people with whom one must cooperate in facing the situation—whether in a marriage or in a corporation—the key to cultivating moods is the revision of these assessments: understanding through conversation just how others see the situation and, just as important, how they see you and your role in the situation. Conversation leads to mutual understanding, and understanding should lead to resolutions and engagements, actions that will bring about new situations and open up new possibilities. Bad moods and distrust flourish in the shadows, in privacy, in situations defined by "divide and conquer" strategies. The bright light of conversation shows them for what they are, and it is perhaps our shared optimism that tells us that most of the time, the bad moods cannot be sustained in the daylight or in public once we have truly resolved to come to trust.

The exception, perhaps, is what we have called cordial hypocrisy, that veneer of courtesy and amiability that is presented as a good mood, supposedly conducive to good morale. But managers in such ostensibly happy organizations often hate and complain about their jobs even more than those in companies with overtly bad moods. Moreover, even a slight probing of this pervasive good mood discloses a more deeply pervasive mood of despair, resignation, or resentment. A few hours' consulting is usually more than enough to bring this dark mood bubbling to the surface (at which point some of the most cordially hypocritical managers will insist on the pointlessness of the exercise). Cordial hypocrisy at its worst is a collective form of self-deception and denial, and thus immune to easy resolution. It is the most dangerous antithesis to authentic trust because it insists on believing that it *is* authentic trust. But its resistance to change is a conclusive demonstration that this cannot possibly be the case.

Moods and emotions are not merely personal. They are often shared and social, and they close off possibilities and disrupt our working with others. Moreover, our moods and emotions do not happen to us. We choose them. To think of trust as an emotional phenomenon is to accept that trust begins (and ends) with care, and it is also to embrace the idea that trust is a personal choice and within our realm of responsibility. This suggests a philosophy of life. Human life is a series of emotional engagements and projects, in which we invent a shared future through our moods and emotions. To believe otherwise is to cut ourselves off both from other people and from the power we each can bring to our lives by working together and trusting one another.

Trust as Background and as "Medium"

If authentic trust is trust articulated and carefully considered, then it is important that we come to understand how it is that trust tends to recede into the background and become more or less invisible, taken for granted in our everyday relationships. Simple trust never emerges from the background and remains (by its very nature) unreflective. But authentic trust cannot and does not constantly occupy our attention either. Once people embark on a trusting relationship, they have much else to work on and think about. If we are to understand authentic trust, we must understand this notion of trust as background.

It is trust as background that gives rise to all of those "substance," "stuff," and "medium" metaphors. Trust becomes invisible (or transparent) in many (even most) trusting relationships precisely because it becomes part of a pervasive mood, and as a mood, it tends to provide the background rather than the focus of our activities. But that doesn't mean that trust has become either simple or blind. It remains active in the background; our interpersonal practices go on largely through more or less habitual routines and unthinking (that is, unreflective) exchanges and conversations. Trust thus appears to be something like a medium or framework *within which* cooperative activities become possible. There is something to be said for this view (with all its metaphorical variations), but it must ultimately be rejected because it conflicts with our consciousness of trust as a dynamic, reciprocal, emotional relationship, a many-faceted social practice.

The general problem is that we tend too quickly to assume that complex human practices are by their very nature "conscious" or "reflective" —that is, that they are at the forefront (or at least the perceptible periphery) of consciousness, matters of attention, or at least dim awareness. Philosophers and lawyers insist on this as a matter of professional style, but many people hold similarly Cartesian views about human consciousness—to be conscious is to be self-aware. But much of what we do, and most of what we believe and feel, is not so much in the foreground. It is what some philosophers would call "prereflective," and it is to be found in the background of our activities.[83]

To assume that complex human practices are by nature conscious or reflective, not only articulated but explicitly understood, involves a faulty picture of human life. It is one borrowed, to a certain extent, from some great philosophers, for instance Socrates, who insisted that "the unexamined life is not worth living," and Descartes, who insisted that to exist as a human being ("a thinking thing") was ipso facto to reflect on and to recognize one's existence. But a good deal of human life is prereflective or ontic, as opposed to ontological or self-reflective and articulately self-understanding. Riding a bike, to take a favorite example, involves all sorts of tacit knowledge— "knowing how to" —that cannot be articulated even by most skillful riders. Trust can be treated as a medium (substance, stuff, glue, lubricant, atmosphere) only insofar as it sinks below the threshold of consciousness and escapes our attention. It then seems invisible or transparent only because we do see through it, take it for granted, treat it as if it were just *there*. Trust, in most trusting relationships, slips into the background and is not necessarily the focus of our attention. It then becomes the ground on which we proceed to carry out our cooperative activities. But if it is a ground, then it is a foundation built by many hands. It may seem solid and static, but it is dynamic through and through, and an effort of continuous and changeable will.

Authentic trust remains in the background only until it is stirred into consciousness, typically by the need to make a decision. It may seem invisible, but only in the sense that we are not paying attention to it and are so skillfully engaged in it that we need not attend to or articulate what we are doing. But when establishing trust with someone new—or trying to maintain or restore trust with someone who has breached a trust—none of this can be taken for granted. A person who has once learned to ride a bike no longer pays much attention to the skill itself and is hard-pressed to repeat the instructions. Teaching a child to ride a bike brings these "invisible" skills into focus and forces us to articulate them. At the beginning of a love affair, one might pay careful attention both to what one says and to what is said, to every move and, eventually, every caress. But once established, the conversation becomes much less self-conscious, the caresses become more skilled or at any rate less conscientious (without thereby becoming less meaningful or caring). What was once a matter of keen attention and great concern now slips into the background, where it continues in much the same way as before, but without the attention and explicit concern.

We might follow Heidegger and say that human attention tends to be unreflective until it is shocked into reflection by some sort of breakdown. But this does not make it any less human, or mean that it is a medium rather than an activity. Trust simply appears to be a medium because our attention, once we are resolved to trust, can focus elsewhere. In Heideggerian terms, we might say that the "understanding is not in our minds, but in the skillful ways in which we are accustomed to comport ourselves."[84] Comedians such as Jerry Seinfeld, and good science fiction writers, weave stories of nonsense and horror by simply bringing to light many of these unconsidered default positions. Trust is in the background, but it is by no means a mere backdrop, much less a medium. It is rather that constant way of being through which all forms of engagement and interaction are possible, in which the features of the background are not simply facts or states of affairs but intimately related to the interpersonal activities and emotional interactions at hand.

To talk about trust as background is significant in another way, one that has become particularly important to philosophers in recent years. When an agreement is made explicit, for example in a contract, it is well known that there will always be loopholes and contingencies concerning which the contract is not explicit but on which there will be considerable agreement. Lawyers attempt to close those loopholes and explicitly state those contingencies at their peril, for it quickly becomes evident that there is no end to the possibilities and a contract cannot possibly explicitly cover them all. Philosophers face a similar dilemma when they try to formulate "airtight" arguments and analyses but then find that there are contexts and counterexamples, including rather ingenious circuitous-route-type examples, that thwart the desire for deductive certainty.[85] The concept of the background thus embraces that whole world of merely implicit possibilities and inexplicit premises ("emphymemes") that our articulate and explicit activities tend (rightly) to ignore or take for granted. And in any relationship (or even in a brief transaction), there are possibilities, presuppositions, and "standing conditions" that cannot possibly be brought to our attention.

Like many basic elements of human relationships, trust is recognized mainly in the breach. Trust may be what remains unsaid in the story of a successful relationship; it is the medium in which a successful relationship (and human sociability in general) operates. In such happy circumstances, it is appealing to compare a person living in trust to a fish living in water, oblivious to the water's existence *as water,* as our ancestors probably considered (or did not consider) the air around them. One comes to appreciate the essential importance of air mainly when one is deprived of it. Otherwise, it is as if air is "nothing." (One could tell quite a story about the discovery of air, by the Greeks and by the Chinese. How would an intelligent fish discover water?) But our relationship to the air (and a fish's to water) is neither explained nor exhausted by the idea that it is a medium or the background for all of life's activities. As any physiology student can tell you, our relationship with the air is a complex dynamic with many different aspects, and breathing is one activity that is tantalizingly both autonomic and voluntary. Trust is another: on the one hand one of the most "natural" things we do with people, but at the same time one of our most cautious, deliberative, and responsible concerns. To dismiss trust simply as background or medium is not yet to understand it at all.

Self-Trust, Self-Confidence

We have emphasized the primary importance of relationships and attention to relationships in authentic trust. Accordingly, we have downplayed the centrality of such matters as our reliance on the competence and skills of other people and the idea that trust is some sort of inert "stuff" out of which or on the basis of which relationships are created. But there is a different kind of competence and another essential feature of trust that deserves a different kind of consideration: *self-trust,* the ability to trust oneself to trust wisely and authentically.[86]

Trust is a skill, one that is an aspect of virtually all human practices, cultures, and relationships. Skills are cultivated, whether or not they build on some natural or "inborn" foundation. If we watch a one-year-old babbling and gesturing, we can see that language, although it must be learned, is based on skills that are innate. Watching an infant with its parents and then with strangers makes it equally clear that trust is something learned and cultivated. Trust is a skill learned over time so that, like a well-trained athlete, one makes the right moves, usually without much reflection. Not only trust but the skills that make trust possible recede into the background. We pick up cues; we know when to make requests or offers; we know when to make or not make promises; we feel confident about situations and people because we know and understand the characters with whom we are dealing. Self-trust is confidence in our possession of these skills.

Like all forms of authentic trust, self-trust is always open to reflection and scrutiny. Distrust is not its opposite but its essential companion. Authentic trust is not stubborn resolve.

That seeming self-trust too often turns out to be self-deceptive blind trust. Self-trust includes a healthy skepticism, which paradoxically presupposes the skills and the confidence to trust one's self-critical abilities.[87] Authentic trust is trust that can be confidently subjected to scrutiny. But with this comes the possibility of being wrong. It is by means of such reflection—displayed, for example, in the more innocent jealousy games that lovers play with each other—that relationships are deepened by being made increasingly the focus of care and attention. In authentic trust (as in true love), what changes is not only the confidence one has in the relationship but—just as important—the confidence that one has in oneself in the relationship. What is at stake is not merely the trusting but the whole relationship in which one's trust plays an important part.

Trust as a cultivated skill consists of both "automatic" behavior on the one hand and thoughtful reflection on the other. It is particularly important to emphasize that trust, like most skills, is not learned or cultivated on the basis of *rules*. We are not computers. Trust is a skill to be learned—but by doing, by interrelating, not by following a recipe. There is no proven sequence of steps through which we can make ourselves more trusting or make our employees or children more trustworthy. The way to build authentic trust is to trust. We establish a practice of trusting, a practice that may be different for different people or for different parts of our lives. But because authentic trust has a great deal to do with our own distinctive identity and the creation of a future with other people through which that identity will be transformed, there can be no general recipe for trust any more than there can be a blueprint for the future. As Nietzsche's Zarathustra tells his disciples, "I have found my way. Now you must find yours." Trusting involves an enhanced sensibility that allows us to work and coordinate our actions with other people precisely because we are confident of what we are doing.

We have asserted that trust is intimately tied to self-confidence, but the relationship is not a simple one. Being trusted typically increases self-confidence as well as self-respect, but it can also—especially if the trust is misplaced—undermine it. Trusting someone requires a certain self-confidence, and as is often said, you cannot trust anyone if you cannot trust yourself. We can readily appreciate the sense in which this is true. If you do not trust yourself or your ability to behave correctly in a difficult situation, you may well find it difficult to have faith that others can do so. You also must trust yourself to have a good sense of people, to choose to trust people who are likely to be trustworthy rather than, for instance, because you find them charming or attractive. This is especially true when the task is something we know we are incompetent to perform. We trust a surgeon or a computer technician, for example, precisely because we know we are incapable of performing even the simplest surgery or even the simplest hardware repair. Our self-confidence, as far as our competence goes, is near zero. Nevertheless, our self-confidence in terms of making a good judgment about whom to trust is of the utmost importance. If you do not trust yourself to choose wisely the people you trust or with whom you form relationships, you may have a good deal of trouble trusting people.

A great deal of trust has to do with making *assessments*. An assessment is a statement of opinion, a value judgment, an estimation. It may be based on good, even convincing, evidence, or it may not be. But in either case, it is a statement of opinion. In authentic trust the awareness of the subjectivity of such assessments is essential. Such assessments must not be confused with factual claims, readily confirmable by the evidence. The role of assessments in trust is not limited to our ability to make them and make them well. It also involves our ability to use them to forge a trusting relationship. If you judge that your business partner is irresponsible, that assessment is (or should be) the beginning of a conversation, the beginning of a transformation from distrust or lack of trust to trust. Such conversations are by no means easy or comfortable. But the confident ability to carry on such conversations—whether with your business partner or with your spouse and children—lies at the heart of authentic trust.

Such assessments and conversations are never one-sided.

Authentic trust is created when you come to be unafraid of the negative assessments of people you respect. By the same token, trust is destroyed by flattery or cordial hypocrisy. Flattery becomes an insurmountable block in personal relationships. Cordial hypocrisy is a functional flaw in organizations. Negative assessments, even insults, can provoke authentic trust by breaking through. "Stop being so pig-headed!" may not make friends, but it can be effective in opening up what has been a closed and fruitless conversation. Ideally, such assessments show that you care.

The practice of making and receiving assessments and learning how to negotiate them forms the core of our strategy for building trust in organizations. It also works in troubled marriages, and it may even work with hobbled political economies. But the heart of both the practice and the strategy of building trust is first building self-confidence and self-trust: trust in one's own abilities, skills, knowledge, preparation, and know-how, as well as trust in one's own body and body language, impulses, emotions, self-control, moods, thinking, intelligence, and sensitivity to others. Being able to trust oneself—a phrase that already suggests an odd relationship between oneself and oneself—is so basic that it is almost always left unarticulated in the background in considerations of trust, except, perhaps, on those occasions in which outright betrayal forces it into question.

In discussions of trust, there is usually so much emphasis placed on the intellectual dimensions and strategies of trust (including predictability, probability, and reliance) that hardly any attention is paid to the human body. (Indeed, in this as in many philosophical discussions, such talk seems simply out of place.) But trusting one's own body is the primary form of basic trust, and trusting one's comportment and ability to express oneself—not only verbally but bodily—is a precondition for using the skills for building trust. Think, for example, of the commonplace idea that a person with "shifty" eyes is not to be trusted. Trust in one's own body is, perhaps, a metaphor for self-trust. Even minimally physical activities and practices—typing on a word processor or speaking, as much as running a marathon—presume skills and confidence in those skills that typically come to our attention only when we are first learning them or when they start to break down. When arthritis or muscle cramps set in, when one's fingers are numb from the cold or one's mouth is numbed by novocaine, one's attention suddenly shifts from the object of the act or practice itself—winning the race, expressing the thought—to one's bodily ability to perform the action at all. Anyone who has had his or her legs suddenly give out, or experienced a temporary paralysis or blackout, or walked around with a medical sentence hanging over his or her head (after a heart attack or a cancer diagnosis, for instance) knows all too well what it is like not to be able to trust one's own body. At such times, we remember with wonder what a luxury it was not to have to think about such matters at all. In an athletic event, in dance, or in just plain walking, one trusts one's body to do what it is supposed to do.

Physical trust is, for most of us, a basic form of self-trust. After the initial learning period, such trust is simply taken for granted. But again, what is basic is relative to the circumstances. A person who has grown up with or learned to live with a physical condition may take the condition as given and basically trust that the condition is stable. Where the condition itself is unstable but one is used to it, what is basic may only be one's ability to cope with the uncertainty. Physical trust can serve as a striking metaphor for authentic trust. When we are children, or as young athletes, most of us learn these physical skills with considerable delight and initial attentiveness and then quickly forget about them and about what marvelous abilities they are as they slip into the background of a healthy lifetime of physical activity. When we get older, however, the skills begin to break down. We start to lose what we once took for granted, or pains and impediments make what once was both effortless and "mindless" the focus of renewed and sometimes frustrated, even despairing awareness. But we all know (even if we would like to think otherwise) that this is a natural and inevitable aspect of growing old. We may well rage against the dying of the light, but authentic maturity means accepting it as a necessity.[88] Authentic trust, too, involves getting beyond those years of our lives when trust was simply taken for granted and we trusted ourselves without hesitation to trust wisely and well. As we mature, we come to recognize that trust does indeed take care and attention, and that the focus of that attention must be something more than "getting what we want." It turns, rather, on who we are and what kind of people we want ourselves to be.

Because trust is necessarily discussed primarily in terms of trusting other people, we tend to forget how important it is to trust ourselves. Sometimes trusting ourselves is actually much like trusting another person. We find ourselves waiting to see how we will behave in some emergency or emotionally charged situation, for instance. (Such experiences are sometimes described thus: "It was as if I were watching someone else.") But usually, it is a matter of trusting ourselves to *do* what we have been trained or trained ourselves to do. Some people think that self-trust means the absence of all anxiety, total self-confidence, but they are wrong. Fear and anxiety are indications of uncertainty, and trust necessarily involves uncertainty. It is the *absence* of fear and anxiety that may mark the lack of true self-trust. Their total absence more likely indicates indifference or ignorance, or perhaps a simple trust that is bewildered and devastated when we do fail ourselves.

Knowing Self-Trust

For philosophers, self-trust focuses on one kind of trust above all others—epistemic or "knowing" self-trust. There is a long and distinguished tradition of philosophical literature on this, of which Descartes' rightly famous *Meditations* is the most illustrious example.[89] Indeed, much of philosophy for the past three centuries might well be considered exercises in problematic self-trust, after Descartes. How, Descartes asked, can we trust our own senses? How can we trust that we are not systematically misled? These are heady questions, and it is often pointed out that Descartes did not take them—could not have taken them—very seriously. He was concerned about the problem of justification of our beliefs; he did not seriously doubt his senses or his rationality. But the questions Descartes raised have their everyday analogues, and the virtue of self-doubt that he so highly praised—as opposed to the unthinking acceptance of the commonsense beliefs that surrounded him—is rightly treated as a healthy skepticism for all of us in everyday life. (Imagine for a frightening moment someone who simply believed everything he or she saw and heard on television.)

Self-doubt is not a uniquely philosophical phenomenon. We all rightly wonder whether we know what is going on, even—contra Descartes—what is going on in our own minds. We know that we can make logical mistakes, that our evidence is often hearsay and faulty, that our memories are faulty (increasingly so with age), that our calculations omit essential considerations, that we are sometimes foolish, that our reasoning is sometimes (often?) mere rationalization. Trusting one's knowledge or memory may be a form of reliance, but trusting one's motives and one's own cognitive integrity is truly a matter of trust. The reflection that is practiced by philosophers as a sort of professional duty is actually a sophisticated and usually depersonalized form of the self-scrutiny that we all need to perform from time to time. But although we may be wrong some of the time, we cannot be wrong all the time. (Credit for that logical insight goes more to Abraham Lincoln than to Descartes.) Nevertheless, authentic trust requires continuous self-scrutiny, and such ordinary daily practices as keeping a "to do" list may be an acknowledgment that we recognize the limitations of our own cognitive abilities and, just as important, that we care.

Knowing self-trust is basic and essential if we are to believe anything at all. But, unlike simple trust, this basic trust should never be taken for granted or divorced from a healthy amount of distrust in ourselves. Wisdom is not perfect reason, but, as Socrates taught us, a healthy respect for what we do not know. And that, indeed, is the knowledge basis for trust—not knowing for sure but its opposite, knowing what we don't know, and even knowing that we don't even know what we don't know, and trusting ourselves and other people to help us find out.

Emotional Self-Trust

Because authentic trust is an emotional skill, a set of practices involving our moods, it is necessary to be able to trust our own impulses, moods, and emotions and to be able to trust our own self-control. It is, to begin with, a matter of some concern whether trusting our own emotions and moods is more like trusting someone else, more like reliability, or more like trusting ourselves to think and act in a certain way. Deep questions about selfhood enter into this discussion, questions about whether the emotions are acts of the self, expressions of the self, or alien to the self. Age-old conceptions of emotions as intrusions, as invasions by the beast in us, as transient madness, suggest that our emotions and moods are afflictions and are to be trusted only in the way that we trust the weather, with the added appeal that we can control our emotions and moods (unlike the weather) with chemicals, a proper diet, meditation, and exercises.

It has long been a point of wisdom, in both the East and the West, that the possibility of emotional control lies within us, and that undertaking to get angry or to fall in love is much more like undertaking a campaign or a strategy than like suffering from some affliction. But whatever the analysis, it is clear that we must be able to trust ourselves to be able to control our anger, to control our envy or our jealousy.[90] We trust that our love, once set in motion, will continue, which is not the same as *promising* "to love . . . till death do us part." The promise is one thing, the durability and ability continuously to renew and revitalize the emotion something else, more or less independent of our initial intentions. Any number of contingencies and catastrophes can wreck even the best of marriages, and these clearly are beyond our control.

But notice here that the expression "controlling emotions" is ambiguous. One can control the expression of emotion, the urges and impulses to action that arise out of emotion, without necessarily controlling the emotion itself. Then again, to control the expression is often effective in modifying the emotion, as William James famously observed about a century ago. It is not the expression but the emotion that is often in question in self-trust; we do not want to be angry or jealous or envious. We do not want our love to fade. Can we trust ourselves in this sense, quite apart from our confidence in being able to act correctly and "put on a proper face" so far as anyone outside the relationship is concerned? The answer is that we can, but not by thinking that love is a "force" or a "power" that exists quite independent of our daily practices. Taking love for granted is the surest way of losing it. Making love the authentic focus of our lives and taking care to renew it continuously is the best way of making love last, and the best way of assuring that, even when love does fail, one has truly loved and has not just let it slip away. If we have the self-confidence that we *can* take responsibility for our emotions, we are already halfway to doing so. To think otherwise is to relinquish not only responsibility but any semblance of self-control. We may not be the captains, but we surely are the oarsmen of our fate.

Moods are different from emotion in their pervasiveness, indeterminacy, and openness toward objects. Moods are therefore less attached to any particular occurrence or state of affairs, and they may even seem independent of circumstances. (A great depression or a bout of joyfulness, for instance, may carry over from one situation to the next without noticeable change.) But our moods (and our moodiness) do not simply "happen" to us. We cultivate them through our thoughts and our practices. Nor should we think of moods as only occasional occurrences. We are always in a mood. Moods are our way of being "tuned" to the world. And moods have a good deal to do with whether we are capable of trusting or not. But can we trust ourselves to be in the right mood? And can we do anything about it? We can and must take control of our moods, and we do this by accepting the idea that we *can* take control and by recognizing that how we orient ourselves to the future—rather than simply dwelling on the past—is an essential ingredient in "retuning" ourselves and setting the mood for an authentic trust in which we can help "retune" the moods of others, or of a whole organization.

Trusting our impulses is also an aspect of basic trust. Again, this is a matter on which we may rarely focus. It is one of those forms of trust that comes into view only when it has been betrayed. The most serious cases are those homicidal impulses that afflict a few unfortunate criminal. Some of these impulses can now be controlled by psychopharmacology. Less serious but equally pathological is Tourette's syndrome, in which a patient has an uncontrollable urge to spew obscenities and make comments that the rest of us would certainly edit out of our speech. But we all have impulses that are "out of character," and many of us have impulses that are predictably in character but nevertheless dangerous or destructive or annoying.

For example, most of us have a tendency to become defensive when our work is criticized. This not merely a matter of being offended. It is more often and more significantly a matter of lack of self-trust. Accepting that our work could be improved—and will most likely be improved by the input of others—is a source of true self-trust. Doggedly defending ourselves against the charge of imperfection is a sure sign of lack of self-trust. We may find that we get somewhat jealous when our spouses are heard speaking privately and intimately with others. But to become jealous in such circumstances is not so much a matter of suspicion as it is a sign of insecurity, a lack of confidence in ourselves as partners in a dedicated marriage.

We all have had a rare impulse to do something utterly stupid—jump out a window or scream insults at a police officer. We usually trust ourselves not to have such impulses or, if we do have them, not to act on them. But in the practice of trust, such self-control is utterly essential. The urge to lash out from frustration or to say something harshly cutting in the face of cordial hypocrisy may seem overwhelming at times. But self-control lies at the heart of building trust with others. If you cannot trust your own impulses and behavior, after all, why in the world would you expect other people to trust them, or to trust you when you put your trust in them?

Breaches and Betrayals of Trust

> What he did not know was that Sabina was charmed more by betrayal than
> by fidelity. The word "fidelity" reminded her of her father, a small-town
> puritan. . . . Betrayal. From tender youth we are told by father and teacher
> that betrayal is the most heinous offense imaginable. But what is betrayal?
> Betrayal means breaking ranks, going off into the unknown. Sabina knew of
> nothing more magnificent than going off into the unknown.
>
> —Milan Kundera, *The Unbearable Lightness of Being*

In the background of our discussion of trust, and in the background of every instance of trust, is the specter of betrayal.
Without the possibility of betrayal there can be no trust, only
reliance or predictability. Not all betrayals are equal, however,
and one of the reasons we mistakenly think of trust as so fragile
is that we conflate any number of disappointments or failures
into that one horrific category, the category of betrayal. But
like Sabrina in Kundera's novel, we can see that some "betrayals" are nothing more than "breaking ranks, going off into the
unknown." Trust involves risk, and authentic trust involves
knowingly going into the unknown—together. The consequences of such risks are often disappointment and failure.
That does not necessarily mean that the trust has been
betrayed, or that the trust has been destroyed.

Consider, for a moment, some of the most terrible betrayals
of the twentieth century. The Jews of Europe found it necessary for many centuries to keep their valuables in compact,
easily transportable form—jewelry, for instance—because they
recognized all too well the prejudices and fickleness and consequently the contingency of the human societies they lived
in. They did not trust the people around them, and for good
reason. But with the Enlightenment in Germany, for example,
Jews became more readily accepted and they became more
comfortable. They settled down and called Germany their
home. Many of them firmly supported the National Socialist
party when it came to power in 1933. The result, of course, was
catastrophic. Trust, simple trust, had become a habit. Many Jews
resisted the suspicions whose rationale became all too obvious

in the fast-changing Germany of the 1930s. Their betrayal was the Holocaust, one of those definitive events in the history of humanity that prompts us deeply to examine ourselves (and not just the Germans), and to ask, seriously, whether trust is ever really possible. The answer, we say, is yes, but it must be authentic trust, a willful decision to face the future without naïveté or denial of the catastrophes of the past.

Similarly, the residents of Sarajevo lived together in harmony and trusted their neighbors until 1992, when Slobodan Milosevic fomented civil war and mutual genocide. What had been neighborly trust quickly degenerated into mutual loathing and murder, and the downward spiral of vengeance and vendetta became the logic of everyday life in the city. Croats, Serbs, and Muslims vowed that they would "never again" trust one another, a vow that we hope will turn out to be only an expression of the anguish of the moment and not a true commitment. The commitments that must be made are of exactly the opposite nature: commitments to rebuild trust and never again to allow a Milosevic to stir up such murderous ethnic impulses.

Back in 1956, Chairman Mao Tse-tung famously declared "Let a hundred flowers bloom and a hundred schools of thought contend," attempting to open up an artistic and scientific atmosphere that had become utterly stifled by his repression of all "counterrevolutionary" thoughts and feelings. The world applauded. Chinese artists and intellectuals were rightly cautious, but after Mao published a book of his own "classical-style" poems and the campaign continued (with a speech in February 1957 in which he insisted that only through creative endeavor could China maintain the revolution and elevate political and social life), most of them entered into the new freedom with a sense of enthusiasm. Students at Beijing University started reading Byron and demanding courses on Bertrand Russell. Intellectuals dared political criticism, even questioning Mao. But in June 1957 Mao initiated an "antirightist" campaign, declaring that "he had only let the demons and hobgoblins come out of their lairs in order to wipe them out better." And less than a decade later came the

Cultural Revolution.[91] How many American artists and intellectuals would dare speak up after such an experience? More to the point, how much trust would Americans put in a government that had so betrayed them?

These are instances of massive betrayal. One wonders how societies survive them, but they do. But just as important, such instances do not correspond to the common breaches of trust in our lives, and it is something of a pathology, akin to a mood of paranoia, to react to every disappointment or breach of trust as if it were a full-blooded betrayal. Let us distinguish some of the breaches and breakdowns of trust that are often conflated with betrayal. Keep in mind our overall characterization of authentic trust, trust that focuses not just on a particular outcome but on the relationship as such. An authentic trusting relationship is able to weather all sorts of mishaps and disappointments with no diminution of trust. Indeed, every entrepreneur will tell you, without hesitation, that trusting—whether yourself or anyone else—means first the ability to tolerate and learn from your mistakes. To confuse failure with betrayal is to set yourself up for no creativity, no innovation, no adventure, no intimacy, no trust, no life at all.

The first category of disappointment is simply the category of "things that didn't work out." In technological development, in scientific experimentation, in making a sales call, in making first assignments to inexperienced managers, in going on a first date, there is always a high probability that things won't work out. That doesn't mean that it is anyone's fault. That doesn't mean that one should no longer trust the process, cease research and experimentation, stop making sales calls and wait for the products to sell themselves, stop giving assignments to inexperienced managers (how else will they learn?), or give up on the opposite sex. Here is where trust in oneself, and trust in the practices and processes in which one is engaged, become crucial. And an essential part of those practices and processes is continuing to trust other people—as coauthors and coinventors of the future, as potential good customers, as managers who will learn by doing, as possible mates or possible lifelong friends. "Sometimes things don't work out." That is (or should be) part of our everyday wisdom and acceptance. "Therefore, you cannot trust people." That is the epitome of foolishness.

The second category has to do with mistakes. Sometimes things don't work out and someone is indeed at fault. In the examples above, we recognize the possibility of human error in even the most carefully designed experiment. Salespeople sometimes say the wrong thing, turning off a prospective customer. Managers might at first escape all blame because of their inexperience, but soon we expect them to learn from their failures, and at that point we call their failures *their mistakes*. People sometimes fail in more-intimate circumstances not because "they don't get along" or "were not made for each other" but because they really do misjudge each other's tastes or sensibilities, because they really do say vulgar or stupid things, or because they make the wrong moves or behave clumsily. But to trust people enough to hire them at all means trusting them to make mistakes, and to trust people enough to open ourselves up to the vulnerabilities of intimate behavior means to see beyond the mistakes to the possibilities ahead. Mistakes may be disappointing, and if sufficiently numerous, they can be downright irritating. Occasionally, they may be catastrophic. But focusing on the relationship rather than on the outcome gives us the navigational tools to overcome, if not overlook, mere mistakes. As the Wall Street manager said to his terrified young charge (who had just lost a fortune on the trading room floor), "*Fire you? I just invested ten million dollars in your future with this firm.*"

Among the most important distinctions we can make are those between mere disappointments and mistakes, and between mistakes for which someone is to blame and those for which no one is. In virtually every profession or practice in which there is any real challenge at all, mistakes probably will be made, and some of those mistakes will be mistakes for which someone can be blamed. But blameworthiness does not necessarily signify a breach of trust. What it signifies is the need for negotiation and understanding, the need for further resolve and commitment—in other words, the need for authentic trust.

There are disappointments of trust that might best be attributed to fate. Whether or not there is anyone to blame (and we too often look first for someone to blame), some disappointments are part of our destiny. They may also provide opportunities, but in any case, they are more matters to accept than ones to be railed against, and distinguishing between such matters of fate and matters for blame can be critical to trusting relationships. There are disappointments that happen by chance—the wrong twist of the coin, the wrong card in the hole, being in the wrong place at the wrong time. Sometimes, there is just plain bad luck, and authentic trust consists not in insisting on good luck but rather in seeing beyond luck to the larger picture in which chance plays only a supporting role. For all of the indeterminist marvels of modern quantum physics, the basic truths of our practical universe are still to be found in the dependable ways people behave and what they can do for themselves and each other. And first of all, they can and must trust one another, especially in a world in which luck and chance can never be eliminated.

So far we have considered only those disappointments of trust that involve no blame, or in which blameworthy behavior is sufficiently to be expected that it can and should be overcome or overlooked by trust. But there are blameworthy acts that really are breaches of trust and not mere disappointments. These require something more than looking askance or simply reaffirming commitments. For example, there is that form of incompetence that presents itself as something else: the medical student pretending to be a doctor, the apprentice pretending to be a master, the mechanic who assures you that he can fix your car when in fact he has no idea what is wrong with it or how it might be repaired. The mistakes here are not concerned with the person's competence but rather his or her misrepresentation and fraudulence. The blameworthiness concerns the person's arrogance, insincerity, or lack of self-understanding. And this is no longer merely a matter of making a mistake.

We have entered the realm of apologies and excuses. By apologies, we are not referring to those bits of courtesy that may well be independent of blame, polite expressions of sympathy rather than expressions of remorse. But we also do not mean *mere* expressions of remorse, the verbal equivalent of looking shamefaced or beating one's brow. An apology, like so many of the actions involved in trust and commitment, is a "speech act," not a mere expression but a way of "doing things with words," as Oxford philosopher J. L. Austin put it. An apology can be sincere or insincere. It can be well timed or too late. (Or, sometimes, suspiciously too early.) It can be appropriate or inappropriate. And as a speech act, it is not merely a way of expressing one's feelings but a way of initiating a conversation, a bit of negotiation. The most desired replies are "I forgive you," "Forget it," and "No problem." But to think of an apology as a sort of social magic wand, for which forgiveness is automatic and assured, is itself a serious misunderstanding and a betrayal of trust. To assume that one's apology erases the error for which it has been issued violates the trusting relationship, which is that one will take seriously and try to make amends for one's errors. An apology is a statement of an intention to redeem oneself, and the beginning of a conversation about how this can be done.

We should also be wary of excuses as responses to mistakes and breaches of trust. Jean-Paul Sartre famously fashions his entire philosophy around the notion that *there are no excuses*, that we are ultimately responsible for everything we do and what becomes of us. Taken at full strength, this is perhaps an overdose of the antidote to current victim psychology, which finds excuses for everything (if not in one's upbringing, then in one's circumstances). But the need for such an antidote is evident enough, and that antidote is a healthy sense of responsibility. With this in mind, we should be wary of those who automatically make excuses when they would be better off looking for solutions, who shift the blame to someone or something else instead of trying to face up to the damage they have done and the best ways in which it can be repaired.

A different kind of breach of trust is indifference, a lack of sufficient caring. This may manifest itself in simple inattention, but it may also be shameful disregard. A doctor who does sloppy work or remains indifferent to progress in his specialty is blameworthy, but a surgeon may perform an operation perfectly, but by being inattentive to the emotional needs of her patient nevertheless breach the trust between them. Just as care is an essential ingredient of trust of every kind, lack of caring and indifference stand as antitheses to trust. Cynicism, even when it presents itself as serious and sincere, is often a self-deceived form of indifference. One pretends not to care when one really does care, or one intends not to care because one does not want to be responsible for doing anything about the situation. But between cynicism and indifference, there is only a philosophical difference: the cynic claims to have a philosophy of life to justify his or her irresponsibility.

Insincerity gives rise to many breaches of trust, on several different levels. One may be insincere in making a commitment or a promise, and the entire relationship may be undermined from that point on. Similarly, one may make an insincere offer, with no intention of seeing it through, hoping perhaps that the recipient will forget about it, or be too polite to follow through, or too timid to file suit or seek other recourse. One can even be insincere in making requests (for instance, in requesting information or advice that one doesn't need), thus causing the other to believe in a bond that really does not exist, or even initiating a kind of mockery. (Thus cynicism, in its more vicious forms, is also a kind of insincerity.) But having made a sincere commitment, one may nevertheless be insincere in one's dedication to seeing it through, or one may lie about its progress or outcome, probably making excuses along the way. Here we are past the mere "blameworthy mistake" category of disappointments and well into serious breaches of trust. From here, genuine betrayal is only a stone's throw away.

Lying is in itself a breach of trust; indeed, by some standards, the ultimate breach of trust. Lying embodies a wholesale insincerity—stating as truth what one fully knows not to be true—and it may also manifest a profound lack of caring, even when the lie (a "white" lie) is intended to protect the feelings of the person to whom the lie is told.[92] In such cases, one may well care about the feelings of the person, and that is a form of care. But it is a shortsighted, limited notion of care, and it may cause violence to the longer-term relationship. ("If you would lie to me about a little thing like this, how in the world can I ever know when to believe you?") But many lies are not so white, and not intended to protect the feelings of the recipient. They are rather designed to protect the liar from the consequences of his or her actions. Thus Kant, in a judgment that captures the viciousness of some lies, says that lying is a violation of the very humanity of the person lied to, a denial of his or her human dignity. Harsh words indeed, but it is no accident that virtually all the major thinkers of the Western tradition, from Aristotle to Aquinas to Kant and even to Nietzsche (who prided himself above all on his honesty), have condemned lying in the most unambiguous terms.

Reneging on one's promises is a clear case of a breach of trust, but here as always we must be careful to look at the larger picture and not just at the singular performance. Sometimes one fails to perform according to one's promises for any number of reasons we have already considered: because of circumstances, bad luck, the intervention of fate, the failure of other people to come through on *their* promises. There are legitimate excuses, although many excuses are a matter of irresponsibility and the desire to escape the consequences of one's actions, and not everything that seems to be an instance of reneging is a violation of trust. For example, one sometimes makes a promise but never gets the opportunity to warn the person who trusted one that the conditions have changed. The promise may no longer be performable. In retrospect, that should surely be treated differently than the case of someone who makes a promise insincerely or quite intentionally decides not to honor his or her word. Promises can be renegotiated in process, not necessarily because of changed circumstances but perhaps just because the ones who make promises come to realize that they "bit off more than they could chew" and rightly decide that the sooner they come clean, the better. This is not a matter of betrayal but its opposite, a further confirmation of trust. Again, the lesson to be learned is that not all disappointments and unfulfilled commitments are violations of trust. What makes trust strong and vital is its flexibility and its attention, not only to the consequences, but to the relationship that trust helps create and the possibilities it thereby discloses.

Breaches of contract should be considered along the same lines. On the one hand, irresponsible indifference to contractual obligations should surely be treated as the most explicit (and legally liable) form of betrayal. But not all breaches of contract fall into this category. One American bank had an elaborate set of arrangements with a Japanese bank, and those arrangements were for the most part defined by and entangled in a morass of contractual agreements. When the Japanese economy hit hard times and the real estate market (in which both banks had heavy liabilities) collapsed, the Japanese, in effect, threw the contract to the wind. The American lawyers were outraged, but the Japanese response captured a good deal of what we have been saying here. The Japanese said, We don't view contracts as sacred. We view the relationship between us as sacred. In times of desperation, friends do not enforce contracts but look to the needs of the other and the long-term relationship.

That is authentic trust. And what counts as a breach of contract or a breach of trust more generally should always be considered within that larger framework. It is a question of always keeping in mind what really counts.

Trust, Hope, and Forgiveness

Maintaining authentic trust in relationships and organizations can easily become a routine matter, a continuing sequence of commitments and their satisfaction. Trust readily slips into the background and may well appear to be no more than the "atmosphere" or "ethical substance" of ongoing transactions. Building trust, by contrast, takes more-focused attention, an escalation of commitments, some talk about trust and a good deal of transparency (sincerity and honesty) with regard to most transactions. But the hardest cases for authentic trust, the situations in which all hope of trust is likely to be lost, are the tragedies of trust destroyed, whether suddenly, in a single massive betrayal, or slowly and systematically over the years, in that familiar downward spiral of distrust that has become so painfully evident in the world today.

Restoring trust, building trust on the ruins, seems like a hopeless enterprise. The essence of betrayal, one might suggest, is the utter destruction of trust. But the reason that we question many of the common metaphors for talking and thinking about trust is that it is by no means obvious that trust can actually be "destroyed." If trust were a particular sort of stuff or substance, or if trust were a particular kind of arrangement or structure, then metaphors of destruction would make literal sense. Simple trust, precisely because of its simplicity and innocence, can be destroyed. (Innocence lost is gone forever.) But insofar as trust is authentic and has already taken account of the possibilities of betrayal, insofar as trust is part and parcel of the ongoing dynamic of a relationship—even a relationship between enemies—it remains an open question and a continuing possibility.

Mutual need, for instance, often forges at least tentative trust in the place of enmity, in the face of a common enemy. (The obvious moral of H. G. Wells's *War of the Worlds,* and any number of science fiction novels and films, is the need for the warring nations of Earth to unify against an extraterrestrial attack.) Sometimes time alone smooths over the rubble of a once virulent enmity and makes possible the growing trust that routine and familiarity may breed. People do forget. Or their stories change with time, not always in the direction of exaggerated hostility. Sometimes the original reasons for hatred and hostility dwindle into the twilight of time, rendering ongoing animosities irrelevant. Sometimes a single incident intervenes, perhaps a Romeo and Juliet tragedy involving two young people from opposite sides of the divide.

All of these solutions to the problem of endemic distrust and betrayal depend on factors that are out of our hands, on the involvement of a third force, on the slow passing of time. But there are two ingredients in our possession that make the restoration of trust possible. They are the mood of *hope* and the complex act of *forgiveness*.

The concept of hope has received a good deal of attention in the context of religion. It has received less attention as a concept intimately tied to trust. In one sense, the connection should now be self-evident. If authentic trust and the moods in which it is entangled are oriented toward future possibilities (rather than dwelling or depending on the past), then, like hope, authentic trust can be defined in part in terms of its positive attitude toward the future. One might call this optimism, but optimism suggests that things will work out well, whereas we want to insist on our positive contribution to how things will work out, by way of what we do, and because of our deciding to trust others to do it with us. Second and third marriages have been described by caustic wits as "the triumph of hope over experience." Cynicism aside, this is a fair description of authentic trust, assuming, that is, the love in question is not simply blind. The notion of optimism also suggests lightheartedness; "always look on the bright side of things." But hope, like authentic trust, need not be quite so Mary Poppinsish. Hope can be fully aware of the dangers and obstacles in its way, and authentic trust, as we have characterized it, is essentially alert to the possibilities of betrayal and the reasons for distrust.

Without hope, there is little reason to trust. That is why we said that despair (another forward-looking mood, but one that always looks only on the dark side of things) is antithetical to authentic trust. It is the opposite of hope. Resignation is also antithetical to hope, but it is more backward looking, conflating disappointments in the past with the inevitability of the future. But hope too is often presented as a rather desperate reaction, as hanging onto a thread in the face of probable disaster. It is thus important for our discussion of trust that we understand the ways in which hope can be invaluable, not only in the face of disaster but as an ongoing theme in our lives. After all, to quote Lord Keynes, "In the long run, we're all dead." But that doesn't mean there is no hope, even without raising the possibility of an afterlife. There is always hope *within* our lives—for as long as we are alive. There is hope for our children and our grandchildren, and for future generations everywhere. There is hope for our projects, for our dreams, for humanity. And there is always hope for our relationships and the restoration of trust, just as long as we believe there is.

It may be possible to have too much hope, but in most such cases the hope might better be described as unrealistic ("blind hope"?), as self-defeating hope. (In Stephen King's short story "The Shawshank Redemption," Red tells Andy, "Hope is a dangerous thing, hope can drive a man insane, has got no use on the inside.")[93] Or hope may be merely an excuse ("If I *hope* for this, then I will not have to *work* for it"). In prison (as King suggests in his story), hope keeps a person alive. In relationships, in a marriage, hope keeps the daily routines of domesticity from rendering the romance routine. For an entrepreneur, just setting out on a new and exciting road, hope provides the incentive, the motivation, even the path itself. Hope, like entrepreneurship itself, does not have a road map to the unknown. There are no rules to follow. (The rules sometimes laid down by famous entrepreneurs *after* their success are almost always misleading. It was the lack of established rules, the absence of a map, that made their success possible.)

Hope, unlike strategy, has no particular plan. It may not even have any particular outcome. For a married couple, the hope is for a happy life together, for children and their happy lives, but as most successful couples and virtually all parents know (at least in the advanced industrialized societies), blueprints for the future are at best ossifications of hope. So too in the successful corporation. Not only individual entrepreneurs but whole companies, in these days of rapid transformation, must learn to see the future not in terms of strategic planning but in terms of open possibilities, possibilities heretofore unimagined and therefore impervious to strategies that we can now devise. The all-too-familiar response of a great many companies, however, especially those with hierarchies and operations firmly set in the past, is some form of panic and confusion, often ending in despair. The possibilities of the future give rise not to hope but to denial, thus closing down those possibilities instead of opening them up. And opening up possibilities is what hope and authentic trust are all about.

In the restoration of trust, hope is the essential ingredient. Havel's plea to the Czechs—"We have to learn to trust one another"—was not only a plea for trust but an expression of hope. Negative thinking, which had become so much a part of the Eastern European temperament, militates against hope. ("But suppose it doesn't work out?" or worse, "These things never work out.") Positive thinking, the holding open of hope for a different and as yet unknown future, was an unfamiliar experience. After fifty years of oppression and a Soviet policy that quite malevolently set Czech against Czech and family against family, trust had to be rebuilt—indeed, perhaps even created for the first time—from the psychological rubble of a ruined empire. The first step in that rebuilding, and the definitive one (still not adequately realized), is hope.

Forgiveness plays a particularly dramatic role in the restoration of trust. Whereas hope sets the mood, forgiveness is the instrument, the social practice (with its many cultural variations) that makes renewal possible. Forgiveness is a direct response to betrayal. It is especially important to emphasize that forgiveness is an action—or a sequence of actions—and not simply a state of mind. It is, by its very nature, a reaching out to the world, specifically a reaching out to the betrayer and a ritualized undoing of the act or acts of betrayal. Forgiveness does not always have to be verbally articulated and formally expressed in the public realm, but, in practice, this is what happens. One can indicate that one has forgiven a betrayal, for instance, by simply acting toward the betrayer as if there is nothing wrong, although this carries with it the liability that such behavior may well be interpreted as mere artifice, to trick the betrayer into lowering his or her defenses before getting even in some equally hurtful way. Or the absence of explicit forgiveness may indicate that the person betrayed simply does not take this particular betrayal—or the betrayer—seriously, which may constitute an offense in its own right. For such reasons, an explicit verbal act, paradigmatically some form of "I forgive you" or "Forget it," is particularly desirable.

This ritualized aspect of forgiveness is often ignored or confused. Forgiveness, because it need not be formally articulated, is often taken to be a merely mental act or the initiation of a state of mind. One supposedly puts oneself into a frame of mind in which the offense, the betrayal, is no longer considered of significant importance. It is thus a way of setting oneself up to continue the prebetrayal relationship, a preliminary to getting ready to go on. This has some truth to it, but the mistake is metaphorically putting it all "on the inside," as a subjective act of mind rather than as itself an essential part of the relationship, like the trust that was betrayed. Such states of mind do exist. Forgetting is one of them. "Forgive and forget" make up a familiar duo, but we should ask why one needs to do both. Isn't forgetting alone sufficient? If one doesn't even remember the betrayal, what is there to forgive? One might argue that to forgive and not forget is to keep the betrayal alive, to leave it in an active though latent mode, ready to hand should future breaches of trust call for its use. True, but why should we take forgetting—which in such cases is often a species of denial or self-deception—as a particular virtue? The betrayal has now become part—very likely an essential part—of this relationship and its history. Forgetting it is not likely, nor is it particularly commendable. What is both a virtue and compatible with the living truth of the relationship is the public act of forgiving: putting the betrayal behind us but not out of mind, and moving on.

But moving on through forgiveness does not imply a simple return to what once was. In the case of a betrayal of simple trust—trust that had always been taken for granted—there is no return to that state of innocence, and trust (now authentic trust) will always be guarded by an appropriate amount of caution. In the case of a betrayal of blind trust, it is highly unlikely that the victim will allow himself or herself to be quite so blind again, or, if that happens, the self-deception will now have to be ratcheted up to a new and possibly pathological level of denial. In the case of a betrayal of authentic trust, however, the betrayal is never entirely unexpected, and so one might even say that it is more of a disappointment than a full-blooded betrayal. But this, perhaps, treats the betrayal too lightly and lets the betrayer off too easily. The betrayal of authentic trust is still a betrayal, even if to some degree anticipated. And the betrayal of authentic trust leads, accordingly, to a profound alteration of the trusting relationship. Forgiveness is one way to restore trust, but it will probably not return the relationship to its former state. Nevertheless, if the betrayal is placed firmly in the past, overcome (but not erased) by forgiveness, authentic trust may thereby be deepened, the commitments on each side strengthened, and the mutual attention paid to the relationship increased in a way that will improve the lot of both parties.

By contrast, consider one of the most familiar alternatives to forgiveness—revenge, or "getting even." One might say that the natural response to betrayal is to do some sort of harm in return, "measure for measure," or, in the less flattering phrase adopted by Socrates, "the exchange of evil for evil." Indeed, one might even argue that forgiveness is possible only in the light of revenge, with revenge as the obvious alternative. This has a certain truth to it, but it also involves a certain confusion. The truth is that forgiveness does recognize the appropriateness of revenge in exchange for betrayal, but then moves beyond it. The confusion is that the abstention from rightly deserved punishment is not necessarily forgiveness but *mercy*. But one can be merciful without being forgiving, just as one can forgive without forgetting. Mercy is the suspension of punishment; forgiveness is the cancellation of the *need* for punishment. Nevertheless, some sort of punishment by way of revenge stands as the obvious and sometimes (and in some cultures) seemingly mandatory response to betrayal. Forgiveness must be understood against the background of punishment and revenge. In the absence of a warrant for punishment (whether or not one *wants* to punish), there would be nothing to forgive.

Resentment is another poor alternative to forgiveness, but it is by no means so straightforward. It is similar to revenge in its desire for vengeance, but it is different in its actual strategy. Revenge is quick—indeed, sometimes almost instantaneous. (When it is immediate, it might better be viewed as *retaliation*.)

Resentment tends to be slow and simmering, steeped far more in the dream of vengeance than in its actuality. That is precisely what makes resentment so dangerous, for whereas revenge can sometimes indeed restore the balance and provide a level playing field on which to restart negotiations and renew mutual understanding, resentment, because of its clandestine and defensive nature, does not allow for that opportunity.

Forgiveness is the most virtuous and judicious of the responses to betrayal, but this does not mean that forgiveness is undertaken only for its own sake or because it is the right and moral thing to do. Forgiveness may itself be strategic, or it may simply be the obvious way to optimize the good for all. Attempted revenge may well misfire, leaving a score that has yet to be settled. Or one can overdo revenge, give more than measure for measure, inviting retaliation or more vengeance in return. And because the "measure" in question is largely dependent on the satisfaction of the aggrieved parties, even what might be viewed (from some more neutral point of view) as fit and justified revenge may not be perceived as such by the recipient. At its worst, this can lead to vendettas and increasing distrust. On the other hand, forgiveness implies a certain largesse on the part of the forgiver, and in addition to allowing the relationship to move on it may therefore provide special benefits and increased status to the one who had the "bigness of heart" to forgive a betrayal instead of punishing it.

There are other alternatives to revenge and forgiveness, and it is worthwhile to mention them here, if only to indicate the richness of the possibilities for getting beyond betrayal and restoring trust. There is compensation, although this is easily confused with punishment (especially given the legal notion of "punitive damages"). Compensation is repayment, where the betrayal consisted of some quantifiable good. Money is the most obvious example. When the betrayal is financial, as in many securities fraud cases, the idea of "measure for measure" would seem to have a precise meaning. Compensation in this sense could thus be assimilated to the more general concepts of debt and repayment. That would be misleading, however, because what must be compensated for is not merely the

financial loss but also the betrayal. Thus the apparent quantita-
tive objectivity gives way to something much more subjective. And when the loss due to the betrayal is entirely made up
of such intangibles as pride, status, self-confidence, and trust,
the notion of compensation begins to look troublesome
indeed.

But this is so only so long as we continue to ignore the
essence of authentic trust, which is not merely the confidence
that one will be repaid but the willingness to engage in conversation and negotiate with the betrayer. Again, the difficulty
with understanding betrayal, as with understanding trust, is our
tendency to see trust as a psychological attitude toward
another rather than as engagement in a relationship. Compensation thus becomes an *intersubjective* question, and it can be
settled not by appeal to some objective standard or rule but by
the agreement of the parties concerned. Such a conversation
or negotiation may not proceed easily, comfortably, or without
rancor. But in (supposedly "primitive") societies where there is
an established practice of "buying off anger" in the case of
betrayal, a great deal of violence is prevented and the payment
of the agreed-upon amount (in goods or other compensation,
including work and, in some cases, even slavery) in effect can-
cels out the betrayal. One might speculate that the reason some
"advanced" societies suffer from such grotesquely overloaded
court dockets and prison facilities is precisely because those
who betray others insist on maintaining the other as "other,"
someone to be "dealt with" rather than talked to and negotiated with.

There is another alternative to revenge as a response to
betrayal that is easily confused with forgiveness, but it is significantly different. One might call it genuine empathy, but the
idea is not just that one "feels with" the betrayer. Indeed, it is
hard to imagine exactly what that would mean. One might,
with a huge stretch of the imagination, imagine how in a similar position one might also betray someone (namely oneself, in
this imagined case). But it is precisely because such an act of
imagination is so difficult that the betrayal counts as a betrayal
in the first place. (If it were simply a matter of "I would have

done what you did," then it is not so much trust betrayed as an unfortunate case of "the shoe being on the other foot.")

It is the nature of betrayal that one is caught in a dramatic asymmetry; the person betrayed is *not* in a position to identify easily with the betrayer. Better to say "We're all in this together," not so much out of a concern for the general good (which may be an excellent reason for forgiving) but because one refuses to put the other in the place of "other" and instead resolves to listen and understand. This may or may not lead to forgiveness, but it will usually reduce some of the mutual suspicion and antagonism. And where the breach of trust is something less than full-blown betrayal, as it usually is, empathy, understanding, and good listening may be the perfect ways to prevent future misunderstandings and mistakes. How often are breaches of trust due to just such misapprehensions of what was really expected, or when it was expected, or how it was to be done? Listening is the other ingredient missing in a good deal of the talk about trust. Authentic trust is a matter not simply of having the right attitude or perspective but of participating with others in forging a genuine relationship. Appreciating others' weaknesses and concerns is as important as being aware of the possibility of betrayal and being willing to forgive. Forgiveness, like authentic trust, should be conceived of and practiced as participatory, not just a matter of attitude.

Authentic Trust and Leadership: Disclosing New Worlds

The old paradigm of trust is simple trust, that perfectly ordinary trust that quietly slips into the background of comfort and familiarity. The new paradigm of trust is authentic trust, in which the question of trust is front and center, in which commitment and not comfort is the critical concern, in which the promise is not mere security but innovation and adventure. Ordinary, unreflective trust in a marriage may be fine for getting through the day, but a marriage also captures romance when daily domesticity is no longer the focus, when the essential ingredient is the future, which brings with it change, growth, and the dramatic development of a shared identity.[94] Authentic trust in marriage provides a great deal of freedom for expression, for exploration, for experimentation. It is not simply caught up in the present; it is open and reaching for a future together. It is appreciative and romantic about the past. (The word "romantic" means, among other things, "storylike.") A marriage based on authentic trust is an adventure, a work of art. Thus authentic trust is extraordinary in that it goes beyond the immediate and the familiar. It is not merely a comfortable way of living in the world. It discloses new worlds, a far more exciting venture than the usual "happily ever after" ending of the merely fictional romance.

Authentic trust in business and politics provides ample opportunity for complex and cooperative projects that otherwise would have been unthinkable. But in the realms of business and politics, authentic trust opens up a special role for *leaders,* those who exemplify the art of trusting and inspiring trust. In ordinary times, leaders might just as well be managers or administrators, people who are "in charge" in only the limited sense of coordinating and motivating routine and familiar patterns, leading to a predictable and therefore "manageable" future. But when the world is rapidly changing, managers and administrators tend to be dead weight, holding down an organization's center of gravity, perhaps, but also, inevitably, holding the organization back. The notions of "normal" life and "business as usual" are, for most people, nostalgic reminders of a lost time. Life at the turn of the millennium is not uncomfortable, but it certainly is not secure in any sense that our ancestors (or even perhaps our grandparents) would have recognized. Now, new worlds are opening up before us all the time, because of new technology, because of the new "multicultural" sensibility, because of the global economy. These new worlds are not unfamiliar, but what is familiar is always changing rapidly. Certain features of friendship, family relations, romance, and community may seem perennial, but even in these hallowed realms the times are changing. In business and in politics, the only thing that it is safe to predict is that in ten years' time, the world will be radically different, and we need leaders, not managers, to take us there.

Who is a leader? What do leaders do? These questions are often muddled by the notion of *power,* as if a leader is simply one who has power (of office, of the electorate, of the army). But such leaders, even when they are well meaning and not corrupt, often turn out to be no more than managers, although perhaps particularly forceful managers. They tend not to change things (in particular, whatever it is that provides them with their power), and they tend to get stuck in their own status quo. (Even Hitler's imagined "Thousand-Year Reich" was a model of static endurance, not of progress and change.) But leadership, as opposed to mere power, requires trust, the trust of others to be led into not only an unknown but an adventurous future.

The "Who is a leader?" question also gets sidetracked by the mysterious notion of *charisma.* Theorists since Max Weber have suggested that charisma (which literally means "blessedness") is the key to understanding great leaders. We can all think of our own favorite examples. But charisma, whatever else it may be, serves the purpose of clarifying the otherwise ineffable traits of a dynamic leader only by introducing opacities and misunderstandings of its own. Trust is a much better emotional vehicle for any adequate discussion of leadership, and of other relationships too.[95] Charisma places much too much emphasis on the qualities of the leader and too little emphasis on the reciprocal relationships between leaders and followers. In particular, it tends to eclipse or disguise the importance of mutual and authentic trust.

Great leaders do nothing less than alter human identity. The institutions and social patterns that provide the traditional source of ontological security and basic trust are continually disrupted, and if we are not to think of history (in the words of poet John Masefield) as "one damn thing after another," we need someone who will inspire authentic trust in reaching for a new and partly unknown future. This cuts to the very question of who we are. Our individual identities are no longer settled and secured by our origins, our place in our families, our established roles and jobs in society. Whether or not it is true, as Tom Peters and some other social pundits say, that the average person will have ten or more different careers—not jobs but careers—in a twenty-first-century lifetime, it is evident that how we think of ourselves, both as individuals and as members of groups and organizations, is in a state of constant change. And with it, we might say, our conception of what it means to be a human being ("human nature") is in a state of flux. Homer's Greeks looked for leaders who were great warriors, and their paradigm of a human being was a warrior and hero. Through much of the Middle Ages, leaders were spiritual leaders (whether or not they were in power), and thus the ideal of being human was the saint. But how would we describe our dominant paradigms today? It seems to us that any answer would be presumptuous. Human nature, now more than ever before, is what we (collectively) make of it. Great leaders give us a vision of what that will be.

A great leader makes room for something more, something "extraordinary," with rich possibilities for the future. This is "history making," an extension of authentic trust.[96] Whereas authentic trust can go along with established practices, habits, and routines, history making is extraordinary because it reaches far into the future, into the unknown, in the face of even the most traumatic anomalies or breakdowns in our normal routines. In this time of rapid change, in which technology is revolutionized every nine months, in which century-old industries are subject to continuous "restructuring," and in which national borders are in dispute the world over, the line between ordinary and extraordinary authentic trust is increasingly difficult to discern. This need not be traumatic, but neither is it comforting. It requires a different way of thinking about ourselves and about the trust that is necessary to cultivate for the new millennium.

In business, in the new worlds of the entrepreneur, authentic trust is a precondition for success. Entrepreneurs envision the future and, if they are successful, they share that vision. But for entrepreneurs to do this, they must inspire trust, not only in their products or themselves but in the future their product portends. When the Wright Brothers invented the airplane, getting the plane to fly was only the first step in the process; they had to convince the world that the "fast" transportation it had gotten used to only the century before was outmoded and much too slow for the fast-changing modern world. And they were in part responsible for that world. Business may presuppose a foundation of social stability, of ordinary and limited trust, but even once-secure and traditional businesses are now being pushed into unknown territory, in which the products and processes of the future—even just a few years down the line—are becoming matters not only for planning but for speculation.

One can look at some recent nodal points in history, especially the history of technology and politics, for illustrations of this conception of a leader. Authentic leaders do not know what they are doing. What they have is a vision, a direction, and a keen sense of confidence in themselves. What they accomplish is a matter not so much of foresight as of retrospect. The invention of the personal computer, for instance, by Jobs and Wozniak turned out to be an epochal moment in contemporary history, one that has changed all our lives. But during the period in which they achieved their essential insights and did their most inventive work, they were unknown to everyone but their families and friends and had no idea themselves that they were going to revolutionize not only an industry but the way people work and play in this society. Bill Gates's shifting of the world of software from a free-for-all into the world of intellectual property rights began while he was at Harvard, but became apparent only in retrospect, when he had already patented and taken possession of Basic and with it much of the software market in the world. Making it work, however, meant that he had to inspire massive trust in an industry and a set of processes that were just being born. And if he later came to abuse that trust, that only underscores its importance.

In Chinese, there is a single word that means roughly "danger/opportunity." This is an insightful way of thinking about the extraordinary, as both a danger and an opportunity, and it avoids the one-sided, negative interpretation of "crisis" and "trauma." It is difficult to see an event such as a civil war, whether in ancient China, nineteenth-century America, or anywhere else, as anything but a social and cultural catastrophe, much less as an opportunity. Nevertheless, much historical interpretation and writing are devoted to the exposition of the long-term benefits of such catastrophes, and their ability to inspire extraordinary acts of trust and heroism.

The ordinary leader (a manager or an administrator) simply must follow the rules, or follow orders. He or she can follow the way that has already been defined by tradition, or culture, or by his or her predecessors. An ordinary leader can also be innovative, courageous, even adventurous, but the realm in which he or she can be so is already circumscribed, and the right way to proceed is already given. But in times of rapid change, an extraordinary leader has little to follow, for the extraordinariness of the times rests precisely in the lack of guidelines, of stable structures, of unquestioned and unquestionable institutions, of any clear sense of what is appropriate and what is not. The future is open, and there are no right answers (although there are a great many wrong ones). When we think of the most significant political and business decisions of the past several decades, it becomes clear that the challenge was not finding the right answer but deciding between different worlds, whose nature and consequences are by no means clear.

It is this sense in which leaders must *make history,* not in the trivial sense of breaking this or that world record but in the more profound sense of changing the very conditions under which politics, business, and our personal lives can proceed. When Judge Charles Green broke up AT&T and ended its monopoly of the telephone business, it was not clear, nor is it even now, whether this was the right thing to do. We can no longer find out what advantages and harms might have been wrought had Ma Bell stayed a monopoly. Nor do the current success of AT&T as a competitive enterprise and the much lower rates of long-distance telephone service show that the decision was the right one. Taking such action is like falling in love: first one "falls," then one comes to see the world and oneself differently, often in ways one could not have imagined before, and any alternative world becomes almost (but never entirely) unthinkable.

Leadership and trust together provide firm but knowing steps into the unknown. But that is why books on leadership and entrepreneurship (and most books on love) provide so little in the way of instruction, despite the demand. There is no set path to the future, and no recipe for authentic trust. Authentic trust is so particularly geared to the relationship and the situation that no helpful principles are relevant or appropriate. But it is, in the end, the relationship that counts, both for trust and for leadership. We do not proceed in the world alone. To survive and to thrive, we must count on each other and find leaders to follow. Like it or not, we are all in the process of creating a new way of life, and no one knows just what it will be. That is the domain of leadership, authentic trust, and history making.

CONCLUSION
Building Authentic Trust

Why talk about trust? Not only because trust has long been neglected as an essential philosophical and ethical concept, but also because talking about trust is essential to building trust. Even if talking about trust can be awkward or uncomfortable, it is only by talking about trust, and trusting, that trust can be created, maintained, and restored. Not talking about trust, on the other hand, or reducing trust to a mere externality in economic or game-theory treatises, can too easily betray a lack of trust, or result in continuing distrust. Trust is not simply a matter of social or institutional constraints and sanctions. It is not a matter of cultural "atmosphere." And it is not merely a matter of individual psychology ("character") or, more generally, of human nature. It is, and must be made to be, a matter of conscientious choice. We are now too sophisticated to bemoan the loss of simple and blind trust, which may have served humanity well in isolated tribes but became a problem when these tribes came into contact and conflict. What we are now capable of, and what has now become necessary, is authentic trust, sophisticated trust, responsible trust, trust with its eyes wide open.

Building trust presents us with an existential dilemma, one captured well by the German idealist Johann Fichte, who insisted that "the sort of philosophy one adopts depends on the kind of [person] one is." We should by now be tired of the once-bold but now pathological cynicism evident in Thomas Hobbes's oft-quoted view of human life as "nasty, brutish, and short," and more recent "looking out for number one" philosophies. We should also be tired of those whining voices reminding us of human weakness and even "rationality" to explain away and excuse irresponsible behavior. *We believe that philosophy makes a difference.* Believing in the viability of human commitments is the necessary first step in making ourselves trustworthy, and it is the presupposition of trusting as well. To dismiss such commitments in the absence of sufficient constraints is not pessimistic or cynical, much less "realistic," but revealing.

It is still fashionable to be cynical, to dismiss talk of trust as unrealistic, patronizing, and sentimental. But if theorists actually refused to believe in trust and trustworthiness except as probable self-advancing moves in the game of life, we wouldn't trust them to return a book to the library, except, perhaps, with a written contract, a list of assets, and a good lawyer. Cornell economist Robert Frank has done some marvelous ad hominem empirical research in which he has found that economists, who believe as a matter of profession that people act in their own self-interest, leave lousy tips in restaurants, considerably smaller than those left by any of their professional counterparts.[97] His finding, that "economists make bad citizens," might serve as something of a warning concerning trust as well. Thinking about trust in the right way may make all the difference between our being willing and able to trust, on the one hand, and a bad faith refusal to do so, on the other.

NOTES

Introduction

1 These metaphors are taken from Nobel economist Kenneth Arrow ("a lubricant"), Columbia University business professor John Whitney ("glue"), philosopher Sissela Bok ("atmosphere"), best-selling social commentator Francis Fukuyama ("medium"), and sociologist Bernard Barber ("stuff").

2 Recent literature on marriage and relationships often reverses the direction of modeling, suggesting that marriages and relationships are or ought to be construed as business "partnerships." We disagree, and we think this fails to appreciate what is most important about marriage: the trusting relationship. But it also fails to appreciate what is most important about business partnerships: the trusting and extracontractual relationship.

3 Robert C. Solomon, *About Love* (Lanham, Md.: Rowman and Littlefield, Madison Books, 2000).

4 Niklas Luhmann, *Trust and Power* (New York: Wiley, 1980).

5 Annette C. Baier, *Moral Prejudices* (Cambridge, Mass.: Harvard University Press, 1995).

6 Indeed, one of the ways in which trust is destroyed in contemporary civil life is through disagreement about controversial moral issues (abortion, euthanasia, the death penalty, affirmative action)—or worse, about the abstract status of moral principles ("relative or absolute")—even when there is an enormous amount of agreement on the basics ("universals") of decent moral behavior. What the polarized debates over morality seem to ignore is that it is the trust (or lack of it) between the disputants, rather than the terms or outcome of the debate, that determines the quality of life in the polity and the relationships that make it up.

7   Francis Fukuyama, *Trust: The Social Virtues and the Creation of Prosperity* (New York: Free Press, 1996).

8   See Robert C. Solomon, *A Better Way to Think about Business* (New York: Oxford University Press, 1999).

Chapter 1: Trusting Trust

9   Consider Milan Kundera's black comedy about Prague in the 1960s, perhaps with a bit of Kafka as a bitter hors d'oeuvre: Milan Kundera, *The Book of Laughter and Forgetting*, translated by Aaron Asher (New York: Penguin, 1981); Franz Kafka, *The Complete Stories* (New York: Schocken, 1971).

10   Lone Beatle Ringo Starr was more on the mark about trust: "You Know It Don't Come Easy."

11   Daryl Koehn, "Should We Trust Trust?" *American Business Law Journal* 34, no. 2 (1996): 184–203 (a reply to Fukuyama). Koehn points out, for example, that two of Fukuyama's three examples of "high-trust" societies (Germany and Japan, the United States being the third) produced the most destructive and militarily expansionist governments in modern history.

12   See, e.g., Barbara Dafoe Whitehead, *The Divorce Culture* (New York: Random House/Knopf, 1996).

13   Niccolò Machiavelli, *The Prince,* translated by Christian E. Detmold (New York: Airmont, 1965).

14   See Solomon, *A Better Way to Think about Business,* chapter 1.

15   See, for example, Anthony Jay, *Machiavelli and Management* (New York: Holt, Rinehart, and Winston, 1968), and its feminist counterpart, Harriett Rubin, *The Princessa* (New York: Doubleday, 1997). See also Wes Roberts, *Leadership Secrets of Attila the Hun* (New York: Warner Books, 1989). For a critique of such models, see Solomon, *A Better Way to Think about Business.*

16   But those days are past, and now the idea of nuclear disarmament has a new lease on life. See, for example, Jonathan Schell's plea for universal disarmament in *Nation,* February 3, 1998.

17   The distinction between "authoritarian" and "totalitarian," where the former refers to mere brutality and exploitation and the latter adds ideological thought-policing, was made explicit as a matter of American policy by Jeanne Kirkpatrick, starting her meteoric rise to power in the foreign-policy world. Without

addressing the difference between brutality and ideologically motivated brutality, one may simply note that they are just as devastating to community and commerce as they are to personal autonomy and freedom.

18   Karen Jones makes the good but overly neat logical point that trust and distrust are *contraries* rather than *contradictories;* that is, one need not either trust or distrust. One may remain merely indifferent to the outcome. Or one may have "mixed feelings"— that is, one may trust and distrust the same person at the same time (and even in the same respects). See Karen Jones, "Trust as an Affective Attitude," in "A Symposium on Trust," *Ethics* 107, no. 1 (1996): 4–25.

19   Edward Banfield, *The Moral Basis of a Backward Society* (Glencoe, Ill.: Free Press, 1958), quoted in Fukuyama, *Trust,* 97.

20   Jones, "Trust as an Affective Attitude."

21   Friedrich Nietzsche, *Thus Spoke Zarathustra,* translated by W. Kaufmann (New York:Viking, 1954).

22   We want to emphasize that it is the everyday sense of the term *paranoia* that concerns us here, even in its "pathological" state. Some social commentators and authors speak of paranoia as the dominant mentality of modern politics. What they are talking about is not something akin to schizophrenia.

23   Robert S. Robins and Jerrold M. Post, *Political Paranoia: The Psychopolitics of Hatred* (New Haven:Yale University Press, 1997).

24   See Martin Seligman, *The Optimistic Child* (Boston: Houghton Mifflin, 1995).

25   Andrew Grove, *Only the Paranoid Survive* (New York: Bantam Books, 1999).

26   We refer the reader to Peter Sloterdijk, *Critique of Cynical Reason* (Minneapolis: University of Minnesota Press, 1987), for an elaborate if difficult discussion of this social phenomenon.

27   Deborah Tannen, *The Argument Culture* (New York: Ballantine, 1999).

28   Jones, "Trust as an Affective Attitude."

29   Erik Erikson, *Childhood and Society* (New York: Norton, 1993).

30   According to human development theorist Joseph Campos of the University of California at Berkeley, "As with all aspects of infancy, the psychological disposition of trust does not emerge

all of a sudden. Rather, there are gradual accruals that add to a core that in some sense is innate and present at birth" (Letter to Solomon, October 1997).

31   Robert M. Axelrod, *The Evolution of Cooperation* (New York: Basic Books, 1984).

32   R. D. Laing, *The Politics of the Family* (London: Routledge, 1999).

33   John Bowlby, *Attachment and Loss* (New York: Basic Books, 1982).

34   Banfield, *The Moral Basis of a Backward Society*.

35   See also Robert Putnam on intermediary associations and their importance for "civil society" in "Bowling Alone: America's Declining Social Capital," *Journal of Democracy* 6 (1995): 65–78.

36   Bernard Barber, *The Logic and Limits of Trust* (New Brunswick, N.J.: Rutgers University Press, 1974).

37   Dick Morris, *Behind the Oval Office* (New York: Random House, 1997).

Chapter 2: Understanding and Misunderstanding Trust

38   Thucydides, *History of the Peloponnesian War,* translated by P. Woodruff (Indianapolis: Hackett, 1993), 3.83.

39   See, for example, Annette C. Baier, "Trust and Antitrust," *Ethics* 96, no. 10 (1986): 231–60; reprinted in Baier, *Moral Prejudices* (Cambridge, Mass.: Harvard University Press, 1995), 95–129. She sometimes takes simple trust, in particular the trust experienced by babies, as a paradigm. She makes this suggestion to counter the overemphasis in philosophy on relationships between mature, consenting, more or less equal adults. Nevertheless, she does not deny the existence of more articulate and authentic trust relationships.

40   Lawrence C. Becker, "Trust as Non-cognitive Security about Motives," in "A Symposium on Trust," *Ethics* 107, no. 1 (1996): 43–61.

41   Jones, "Trust as an Affective Attitude."

42   This seems to be Russell Hardin's cynical paradigm. Hardin talks extensively about "devices for commitment," for example, which seem to us to amount to *substitutes* for commitment, or simply a denial of what is meant by "commitment" altogether. See Rus-

sell Hardin, "Trustworthiness," in "A Symposium on Trust," *Ethics* 107, no. 1 (1996): 26–42.

43   Becker, "Trust as Non-cognitive Security about Motives."

44   The example is borrowed from Amélie Oksenberg Rorty, "User-Friendly Self-Deception," in *Self and Deception,* edited by Roger Ames and W. Dissanayake (Albany: State University of New York Press, 1996).

45   George P. Fletcher, *Loyalty* (New York: Oxford University Press, 1993).

46   In the movie *One True Thing,* the wife (played by Meryl Streep) accepts just such a compromise in her life, realizing that her life with her philandering husband and her daughter is far preferable to the alternatives. And she never lets on that she knows, aware that an accusation or even an expression of unhappiness might jeopardize the marriage. It is only at the end of the movie, and with constant probing by her daughter, that she reveals that she has known all along.

47   Robert C. Solomon has analyzed this "kangaroo courtroom" scenario in *The Passions* (Indianapolis: Hackett, 1993).

48   Jean-Paul Sartre, *The Emotions,* translated by B. Frechtman (New York: Citadel, 1948).

49   Becker, "Trust as Non-cognitive Security about Motives."

50   Gaia is a relatively recent scientific example in a long multicultural history of such "animistic" conceptions of nature and the earth. In ancient Greece (from which the word *Gaia* is borrowed), in Maori and other South Pacific cultures, in American Indian lore, and in many Asian cultures, the personification of the earth has long standing. (Indeed, it is the conception of the world as "indifferent" that ought to pique our anthropological interest.)

51   This familiar quote is an adaptation from Herodotus. (Thanks to Cynthia Read.)

52   Elmore Leonard, *Rum Punch* (New York: Delacorte, 1982). This novel was made into a film, *Jackie Brown,* by Quentin Tarantino, with Samuel L. Jackson and Bridget Fonda in the relevant roles of Odell and Melanie.

53   See, e.g., Hardin, "Trustworthiness."

54   The more-dramatic versions of this insufficiency are best illus-

trated in the classic example known as Pascal's wager. Blaise Pascal argued that the cost of not believing in God (and consequently going to eternal damnation) obliterated any rational justification for taking such a risk.

55 David Hume, *A Treatise of Human Nature*, edited by L.A. Selbe-Bigge, 2d ed. (Oxford: Oxford University Press, 1888), 269.

56 The best and most philosophical defense of this view, by an accomplished animal trainer (and distinguished poet), is Vicki Hearne, *Adam's Task: Calling Animals by Name* (New York: Random House, 1982).

57 There is a large literature on this. See, e.g., Peter French, "Responsibility and the Moral Role of Corporate Entities," in *Business as a Humanity*, edited by R. Edward Freeman and Thomas Donaldson (New York: Oxford University Press, 1994), 88–97; Manuel G. Velasquez, *Business Ethics* (Englewood Cliffs, N.J.: Prentice-Hall, 1982).

58 French, "Responsibility and the Moral Role of Corporate Entities."

59 The history of the concept of God's grace and its relationship to trust and faith is a fascinating story in its own right. The concept of grace goes back to the ancient Hebrews, and its central thesis is that God is autonomous and without obligation. He can give or refuse to give grace without regard to faith or merit, and although the ancient Hebrews were obliged to trust God, they recognized that they had no right to his grace. Saint Augustine famously argued a similar thesis against Pelagius and denied the relevance of good works to salvation. Similar theses are familiar to us from the Reformation, when Luther and Calvin again emphasized the irrelevance of deeds to earning God's favor. Indeed, Luther initiated the Reformation as a protest against the idea that one could buy (bribe God for) salvation, and Calvin adamantly denied that faith was either a condition or a guarantee of salvation as one of the "Elect."

60 For example, they are conflated by such respected thinkers as Bernard Williams and Niklas Luhmann. Williams, one of the clearest philosophers in the business, resorts to the jargon of game theory. Sucked into the game-theoretical ambit, he finds himself trapped in the paradoxes generated by thinking of trust

as risk assessment, while at the same time (rightly) suspecting that trust can be no such thing. See Bernard Williams, "Formal Structures and Social Reality," in *Trust: Making and Breaking Cooperative Relations,* edited by Diego Gambetta (New York: Blackwell, 1988), 3–13. For a more sophisticated use of this strategy, see Russell Hardin, "Trusting Persons, Trusting Institutions," in *Strategy and Choice,* edited by Richard Zeckhauser (Cambridge, Mass.: MIT Press, 1991), 185–209. See also Hardin, "Trustworthiness," 28.

61 Trustworthiness, on this account, would be what is sometimes called the *formal object* of trust. Anthony Kenny, following Aristotle and the Scholastics, writes of the "formal objects" of various emotions—that is, those objects without which the emotion in question would not be what it is. Thus the formal object of fear might be said to be the fearsome, the formal object of love the lovable, the formal object of anger the infuriating or the offensive or the frustrating. See Anthony Kenny, *Action, Emotion, and Will* (London: Routledge and Kegan Paul, 1963). Ronald De Sousa has suggested that the formal object of humor is "the funny." See Ronald De Sousa, *The Rationality of Emotion* (Cambridge, Mass.: MIT Press, 1987). The formal object of trust might thus be said to be the trustworthy, but a better case might be made for the trustworthy person, or rather a person in a situation who has made certain commitments or who has raised certain expectations and is hoped to be trustworthy.

62 Hardin, "Trustworthiness."

63 Aristotle, *Nicomachean Ethics,* translated by W. D. Ross (Oxford: Oxford University Press, 1948), book 2, chapter 5; Bernard Williams, *Ethics and the Limits of Philosophy* (Cambridge, Mass.: Harvard University Press, 1985), 9. Cf. Aristotle, *Nicomachean Ethics,* book 3. William Frankena, no friend of "virtue ethics," has suggested that the virtues are no more than the disposition to obey rational principles, thus eviscerating the topic as worth study in its own right. William Frankena, *Ethics* (Englewood Cliffs, N.J.: Prentice-Hall, 1973), 64.

64 Plato, *Symposium,* translated by Alexander Nehamas and Paul Woodruff (Indianapolis: Hackett, 1989). See also Robert C. Solomon, "The Virtue of Love," in *Ethical Theory: Character and*

Virtue, edited by P. French, Midwest Studies in Philosophy, vol. 13 (Notre Dame, Ind.: Notre Dame University Press, 1988), and in *The Joy of Philosophy* (New York: Oxford University Press, 1999), chapter 1.

65   Baier, "Trust and Antitrust"; Jones, "Trust as an Affective Attitude."

66   Annette Baier and Laurence Thomas have entered into a special campaign to establish trust as the basis of moral philosophy, in opposition to the still dominant rule- and reason-governed ethical theories. See Laurence Thomas, "Trust, Affirmation, and Moral Character: A Critique of Kantian Morality," in *Identity, Character, and Morality,* edited by Owen Flanagan and Amélie Oksenberg Rorty (Cambridge, Mass.: MIT Press, 1990). Russell Hardin heaps ridicule on those who would "moralize trust," which we frankly find puzzling. Part of what he ridicules is naïve, foolish trust, but to say that a virtue can be employed badly is not to deny that it is a virtue. The alternative he has in mind, apparently, is a rather amoral notion of efficiency and optimality, which we would not be tempted to call "trust" at all. (See Hardin, "Trustworthiness.")

67   Charles Spinosa, Fernando Flores, and Hubert Dreyfus, *Disclosing New Worlds* (Cambridge, Mass.: MIT Press, 1997).

68   The difference between *solidity* and *solidarity* is important here. The former refers to the inhuman, to dense material. The latter refers distinctively to the human, the interactive, even to the spiritual (in the sense that Hegel intended in his use of the word "substance").

Chapter 3: Authentic Trust

69   Barber, *Logic and Limits of Trust;* Patrick E. Murphy and Gregory T. Gundlach, "A Typology of Trust in Business," *New and Evolving Paradigms: The Emerging Future of Marketing,* edited by Tony Meenaghan, *American Marketing Association Special Conference Proceedings* (1997): 596–98. Shapiro, Sheppard, and Cheraskin. "The Grammars of Trust." *Academy of Management Review* 23, no. 3 (July 1998). See also Andrew Wicks, Shawn Berman, and Thomas M. Jones, "The Structure of Optimal Trust: Moral and Strategic Implications," *Academy of Management Review* 24, no. 1 (1998): 99–116.

70   See, for example, Harry Frankfurt, *The Importance of What We Care About* (New York: Cambridge University Press, 1988), and Solomon, *Joy of Philosophy,* chapter 3.

71   For a good discussion of this seeming paradox, see Philip Pettit, "The Cunning of Trust," *Philosophy and Public Affairs* 24, no. 3 (1995): 202–25.

72   Hardin, "Trustworthiness." But see also Christopher Morris, "What Is This Thing Called 'Reputation'?" *Business Ethics Quarterly* 9, no. 1 (1999): 87–102.

73   The phrase "animal faith" came into popular usage with Santayana's powerful argument that trusting relationships—including trust in God—should be understood as something more primitive than social thinkers and theologians were willing to allow. In our terms, what he espoused was simple, inarticulate faith, probably a welcome antidote to the extreme intellectualism he was attacking.

74   See, for example, Annette C. Baier, *A Progress of Sentiments: Essays on David Hume* (Cambridge, Mass.: Harvard University Press, 1995).

75   The "being tuned" metaphor is famously linked to Heidegger, who suggested that mood *(Stimmung),* in particular, is our way of "tuning in" *(Stimmen)* to the world. Martin Heidegger, *Being and Time,* translated by J. Stambaugh (London: Routledge, 1998).

76   See Irving Singer's classic three-volume work, *The Nature of Love,* in which these acts of bestowal and appraisal are analyzed in rich detail. Irving Singer, *The Nature of Love* (Chicago: University of Chicago Press, 1984).

77   This argument is developed in Solomon, *Passions.* For an alternative argument, see Robert Gordon, *The Structure of Emotions* (Cambridge: Cambridge University Press, 1988); Jenefer Robinson, "Startle," *Journal of Philosophy* 42, no. 2 (1995): 53–74; and Jon Elster, *Alchemies of the Mind* (Cambridge: Cambridge University Press, 1999).

78   For an excellent essay on cultivating belief and its relation to trusting, see Richard Holton, "Deciding to Trust, Coming to Belief," *Australasian Journal of Philosophy* 72, no. 1 (1994): 63–76.

79   An excellent discussion of this dilemma is found in Jonathan Bennett, "The Conscience of Huck Finn," *Philosophy* 49, no. 188

(1974): 123–34, in which Huck wrestles with his conscience whether or not to turn in the runaway slave Jim—the course dictated by his racist upbringing—or follow the promptings of his newfound friendship with Jim.

80 Economic metaphors have tended to invade all of psychology, from Freud's overt discussions of "the psychological economy" to current social-psychological interpretations of love as the management of a limited resource. We suggest that the metaphorical infiltration goes instead in precisely the opposite direction.

81 Erich Fromm, *The Art of Loving* (New York: Harper and Row, 1956).

82 See, for example, Solomon, *A Better Way to Think about Business: "The Hypocrite, the Opportunist, and the Chameleon,"* 40–43.

83 The concept of the *background* comes from Heidegger *(Being and Time)* and has been elaborated by Hubert Dreyfus in his *Being-in-the-World* (Cambridge, Mass.: MIT Press, 1997), 75. It has also been analyzed at length by John Searle in his *Intentionality* (Cambridge: Cambridge University Press, 1983), 141–59. "Prereflective" is more commonly used by Heidegger's errant French follower, Jean-Paul Sartre.

84 Dreyfus, *Being-in-the-World,* 75.

85 Some of the best-known circuitous-route-type examples follow the lines of an example offered by Edmund Gettier a few decades ago. Arguing against the standard philosophical analysis of knowledge as "true justified belief," Gettier formulated an example in which someone comes to believe what is in fact true, but on the basis of evidence and arguments that only coincidentally lead to that conclusion. See Edmund Gettier, "Is Justified True Belief Knowledge?" *Analysis* 23 (1963): 121–23.

86 For a difficult formal analysis of self-trust, see Keith Lehrer, *Self-Trust: A Study of Reason, Knowledge, and Autonomy* (New York: Oxford University Press, 1997).

87 See ibid.

88 Reference is made here to Heidegger's notion of authenticity and his emphasis on "Being-unto-death" as our most "necessary possibility." But we have not depended on any of his claims here,

and the picture we present of human life is, we believe, quite independent of any technical philosophy.

89 René Descartes, *Meditations,* translated by D. Cress (Indianapolis: Hackett, 1993). Much more recently, see Lehrer, *Self-Trust.*

90 See Daniel Goleman, *Emotional Intelligence* (New York: Bantam, 1995), for a good discussion of children and adults who cannot control their tempers and other emotional impulses.

91 Jonathan Spence, *The Gate of Heavenly Peace* (New York:Viking, 1981).

92 Sissela Bok, *Lying: Moral Choice in Public and Private Life* (New York: Pantheon Books, 1978).

93 This quotation appears in the context of an excellent discussion of hope: Luc Bovens, "The Value of Hope," *Philosophy and Phenomenological Research* 59, no. 3 (1999): 667-681.

94 Solomon, *About Love.*

95 Jay A. Conger, *Charismatic Leadership* (San Francisco: Jossey-Bass, 1989).

96 On "history making," see Spinosa, Flores, and Dreyfus, *Disclosing New Worlds.*

Conclusion: Building Authentic Trust

97 Robert Frank, T. Gilovich, and D. Regan, "Does Studying Economics Inhibit Cooperation?" *Journal of Economic Perspectives* 7, no. 2 (1993): 159–71.

BIBLIOGRAPHY

Alpern, Kenneth D. "What Do We Want Trust to Be?" *Trust and Business: Barriers and Bridges,* special issue of *Journal of Business and Professional Ethics* 16, nos. 1–3 (1997): 29–46.

Ames, Roger, and W. Dissanayake, eds. *Self and Deception.* Albany: State University of New York Press, 1996.

Aristotle. *Nicomachean Ethics.* Translated by W. D. Ross. Oxford: Oxford University Press, 1948.

Arrow, Kenneth. *Social Choice and Individual Values.* 2d ed. New Haven: Yale University Press, 1970.

Axelrod, Robert M. *The Evolution of Cooperation.* New York: Basic Books, 1984.

Baier, Annette C. "Ethics as Trusting in Trust." In *Great Traditions in Ethics,* edited by Theodore C. Denise and Sheldon P. Peterfreund. Belmont, Calif.: Wadsworth, 1992.

———. *Moral Prejudices.* Cambridge, Mass.: Harvard University Press, 1995.

———. *A Progress of Sentiments: Essays on David Hume.* Cambridge, Mass.: Harvard University Press, 1995.

———. "Trust." In *The Tanner Lectures on Human Values,* vol. 13, edited by Grethe B. Peterson. Salt Lake City: University of Utah Press, 1992. Reprinted as "Trust and Its Vulnerabilities" and "Sustaining Trust" in Baier, *Moral Prejudices,* 130–51, 152–82.

———. "Trust and Antitrust." *Ethics* 96, no. 10 (1986): 231–60. Reprinted in Baier, *Moral Prejudices,* 95–129.

———. "Trusting Ex-intimates." In *Person to Person,* edited by George Graham and Hugh LaFollette. Philadelphia: Temple University Press, 1989.

———. "Trusting People." In *Philosophical Perspectives,* vol. 6, *Ethics,* edited by James E. Tomberlin. Atascadero, Calif.: Ridgeview Press, 1992.

Baker, Judith. "Trust and Rationality." *Pacific Philosophical Quarterly* 68, no. 10 (1987): 1–13.

Banfield, Edward. *The Moral Basis of a Backward Society.* Glencoe, Ill.: Free Press, 1958.

Barber, Bernard. *The Logic and Limits of Trust.* New Brunswick, N.J.: Rutgers University Press, 1974.

Becker, Lawrence C. "Trust as Non-cognitive Security about Motives." In "A Symposium on Trust," *Ethics* 107, no. 1 (1996): 43–61.

Bennett, Jonathan. "The Conscience of Huck Finn." *Philosophy* 49, no. 188 (1974): 123–34.

Blackburn, Simon. "Trust, Cooperation, and Human Psychology." In *Trust and Governance,* edited by Valerie Braithwaite and Margaret Levi. New York: Sage Books, 1998.

Bok, Sissela. *Lying: Moral Choice in Public and Private Life.* New York: Pantheon Books, 1978.

Bovens, Luc. "The Value of Hope." *Philosophy and Phenomenological Research* LIX, no. 3 (1999): 667–681.

Bowlby, John. *Attachment and Loss.* New York: Basic Books, 1982.

Braithwaite, John. "Institutionalizing Distrust, Enculturating Trust." In *Trust and Governance,* edited by Valerie Braithwaite and Margaret Levi. New York: Sage Books, 1998.

Braithwaite, Valerie, and Margaret Levi, eds. *Trust and Governance.* New York: Sage Books, 1998.

Brenkert, George. "Trust, Morality, and International Business." *Business Ethics Quarterly* 8, no. 2 (1998).

———, ed. *Business Ethics Quarterly* 8, no. 2 (1998).

Coady, A. D. P. *Testimony.* New York: Oxford University Press, 1997.

Confucius. *Analects.* Translated by Arthur Waley. New York: Random House, 1989.

Conger, Jay A. *Charismatic Leadership.* San Francisco: Jossey-Bass, 1989.

Cooper, David E. "Trust." *Journal of Medical Ethics* 11, no. 10 (1985): 92–93.

Dancy, Jonathan. "Can We Trust Annette Baier?" *Philosophical Books* 36, no. 4 (1995): 237–42.

Descartes, René. *Meditations.* Translated by D. Cress. Indianapolis: Hackett, 1993.

De Sousa, Ronald. *The Rationality of Emotion.* Cambridge, Mass.: MIT Press, 1987.

Dreyfus, Hubert. *Being-in-the-World.* Cambridge, Mass.: MIT Press, 1997.

Elster, Jon. *Alchemies of the Mind.* Cambridge: Cambridge University Press, 1999.

Erikson, Erik. *Childhood and Society.* New York: Norton, 1993.

Fletcher, George P. *Loyalty.* New York: Oxford University Press, 1993.

Flores, Fernando, and Robert C. Solomon. "Creating Trust." *Business Ethics Quarterly* 8, no. 2 (1998): 205–32.

————. "Rethinking Trust." *Trust and Business: Barriers and Bridges,* special issue of *Journal of Business and Professional Ethics* 16, nos. 1–3 (1997): 47–76.

Frank, Robert, T. Gilovich, and D. Regan. "Does Studying Economics Inhibit Cooperation?" *Journal of Economic Perspectives* 7, no. 2 (1993): 159–71.

Frankena, William. *Ethics.* Englewood Cliffs, N.J.: Prentice-Hall, 1973.

Frankfurt, Harry. *The Importance of What We Care About.* New York: Cambridge University Press, 1988.

French, Peter A. "The Corporation as a Moral Person." *American Philosophical Quarterly* 16, no. 3 (1979).

————. "Responsibility and the Moral Role of Corporate Entities." In *Business as a Humanity,* edited by R. Edward Freeman and Thomas Donaldson, 88–97. New York: Oxford University Press, 1994.

Freud, Sigmund. "Psychoanalytic Notes upon an Autobiographical Account of a Case of Paranoia" (The Schreber Case). In *Three Case Histories,* standard edition, vol. 12, edited by James Strachey. London: Hogarth Press, 1953.

Fromm, Erich. *The Art of Loving.* New York: Harper and Row, 1956.

Fukuyama, Francis. *Trust: The Social Virtues and the Creation of Prosperity.* New York: Free Press, 1996.

Gambetta, Diego, ed. *Trust: Making and Breaking Cooperative Relations.* New York: Blackwell, 1988.

Gettier, Edmund. "Is Justified True Belief Knowledge?" *Analysis* 23 (1963): 121–23.

Goleman, Daniel. *Emotional Intelligence.* New York: Bantam, 1995.

Gordon, Robert. *The Structure of Emotions.* Cambridge: Cambridge University Press, 1988.

Govier, Trudy. "Distrust as a Practical Problem." *Journal of Social Philosophy* 23, no. 1 (1992): 52–63.

————. "An Epistemology of Trust." *International Journal of Moral and Social Studies* 8, no. 2 (1993): 155–74.

————. "Is It a Jungle Out There? Trust, Distrust, and the Construction of Social Reality." *Dialogue* (Canada) 33, no. 2 (1994): 237–52.

————. "Self-Trust, Autonomy, and Self-Esteem." *Hypatia* 8, no. 1 (1993): 99–120.

————. "Trust and Totalitarianism: Some Suggestive Examples." *Journal of Social Philosophy* 27, no. 3 (1996): 149–63.

————. "Trust, Distrust, and Feminist Theory." *Hypatia* 7, no. 1 (1992): 16–33.

Graham, George, and Hugh LaFollette, eds. *Person to Person.* Philadelphia: Temple University Press, 1989.

Gratton, Carolyn. "Some Aspects of the Lived Experience of Interpersonal Trust." *Humanitas* 9, no. 10 (1973): 273–96.

Grove, Andrew. *Only the Paranoid Survive.* New York: Bantam Books, 1999.

Hardin, Russell. "Trusting Persons, Trusting Institutions." In *Strategy and Choice,* edited by Richard Zeckhauser, 185–209. Cambridge, Mass.: MIT Press, 1991.

————. "Trustworthiness." In "A Symposium on Trust," *Ethics* 107, no. 1 (1996): 26–42.

Hearne, Vicki. *Adam's Task: Calling Animals by Name.* New York: Random House, 1982.

Hedman, Carl. "Progressive and Regressive Uses of Reasonable Distrust." *Journal of Social Philosophy* 28, no. 1 (1997): 87–100.

Heidegger, Martin. *Being and Time.* Translated by J. Stambaugh. London: Routledge, 1998.

Hertzberg, Lars. "On the Attitude of Trust." *Inquiry* 31, no. 10 (1988): 307–22.

Holton, Richard. "Deciding to Trust, Coming to Belief." *Australasian Journal of Philosophy* 72, no. 1 (1994): 63–76.

Horniman, Alexander B. "Whatever Happened to Loyalty?" *Ethics Digest* (1989).

Hosmer, Larue T. "Trust: The Connecting Link between Organizational Theory and Philosophical Ethics." *Academy of Management Review* 20, no. 2 (1996): 379–401.

Hume, David. *A Treatise of Human Nature.* Edited by L. A. Selbe-Bigge. 2d ed. Oxford: Oxford University Press, 1888.

Jay, Anthony. *Machiavelli and Management.* New York: Holt, Rinehart, and Winston, 1968.

Johnson, Peter. *Frames of Deceit: A Study of the Loss and Recovery of Public and Private Trust.* Cambridge: Cambridge University Press, 1993.

Jones, Karen. "Trust as an Affective Attitude." In "A Symposium on Trust," *Ethics* 107, no. 1 (1996): 4–25.

Jones, Tom, and Norman Bowie. "Moral Hazards on the Way to the 'Virtual Corporation.'" *Business Ethics Quarterly* 8, no. 2 (1998).

Kafka, Franz. *The Complete Stories.* New York: Schocken, 1971.

Kant, Immanuel. *Lectures on Ethics.* Translated by J. Ellington. Indianapolis: Hackett, 1981.

Kenny, Anthony. *Action, Emotion, and Will.* London: Routledge and Kegan Paul, 1963.

Klein, Melanie. "A Contribution to the Psychogenesis of Manic-Depressive States." In *Selected Melanie Klein.* Edited by Juliet Mitchell. New York: Free Press, 1987.

———. "The Importance of Symbol Formation in the Development of the Ego." In *Selected Melanie Klein.* Edited by Juliet Mitchell. New York: Free Press, 1987.

———. *Selected Melanie Klein.* Edited by Juliet Mitchell. New York: Free Press, 1987.

Koehn, Daryl. "Should We Trust Trust?" *American Business Law Journal* 34, no. 2 (1996): 184–203.

———, ed. *Trust and Business: Barriers and Bridges.* Special issue of *Journal of Business and Professional Ethics* 16, nos. 1–3 (1997).

Kumar, Nirmalya. "The Power of Trust in Manufacturer-Retailer Relationships." *Harvard Business Review* (November–December 1996): 92–110.

Kundera, Milan. *The Book of Laughter and Forgetting.* Translated by Aaron Asher. New York: Penguin, 1981.

———. *The Unbearable Lightness of Being.* Translated by Michael Hien. New York: Harper and Row, 1984.

Lagerspetz, Olli. *Trust: The Tacit Demand.* Dordrecht, The Netherlands: Kluwer Academic, 1998.

Laing, R. D. *The Politics of the Family.* London: Routledge, 1999.

Lehrer, Keith. *Self-Trust: A Study of Reason, Knowledge, and Autonomy.* New York: Oxford University Press, 1997.

Leonard, Elmore. *Rum Punch.* New York: Delacorte, 1982.

Luhmann, Niklas. "Trust: A Mechanism for the Reduction of Social Complexity." In Luhmann, *Trust and Power*, 4–103.

————. *Trust and Power.* New York: Wiley, 1980.

Machiavelli, Niccolò. *The Prince.* Translated by Christian E. Detmold. New York: Airmont, 1965.

MacIntyre, Alasdair. *After Virtue.* Notre Dame, Ind.: Notre Dame University Press, 1981.

————. *Whose Justice? Which Rationality?* Notre Dame, Ind.: Notre Dame University Press, 1988.

Messick, David M., and Marilyn B. Brewer. "Solving Social Dilemmas: A Review." In *Review of Personality and Social Psychology,* edited by L. Wheeler and P. Shaver. Beverly Hills: Sage, 1983.

Misztal, Barbara A. *Trust in Modern Societies.* Cambridge: Polity Press, 1996.

Morris, Christopher. "What Is This Thing Called 'Reputation'?" *Business Ethics Quarterly* 9, no. 1 (1999): 87–102.

Morris, Dick. *Behind the Oval Office.* New York: Random House, 1997.

Murphy, Patrick E., and Gregory T. Gundlach. "A Typology of Trust in Business." *New and Evolving Paradigms: The Emerging Future of Marketing,* edited by Tony Meenaghan, *American Marketing Association Special Conference Proceedings* (1997): 596–98.

Nietzsche, Friedrich. *Thus Spoke Zarathustra.* Translated by W. Kaufmann. New York: Viking, 1954.

Pellegrino, Edmund D. "Trust and Distrust in Professional Ethics." In Pellegrino, Veatch, and Langan, *Ethics, Trust, and the Professions: Philosophical and Cultural Aspects.*

Pellegrino, Edmund D., Robert M. Veatch, and John P. Langan, eds. *Ethics, Trust, and the Professions: Philosophical and Cultural Aspects.* Washington, D.C.: Georgetown University Press, 1991.

Pettit, Philip. "The Cunning of Trust." *Philosophy and Public Affairs* 24, no. 3 (1995): 202–25.

Plato. *Symposium.* Translated by Alexander Nehamas and Paul Woodruff. Indianapolis: Hackett, 1989.

Putnam, Robert. "Bowling Alone: America's Declining Social Capital." *Journal of Democracy* 6 (1995): 65–78.

Roberts, Wes. *Leadership Secrets of Attila the Hun.* New York: Warner Books, 1989.

Robins, Robert S., and Jerrold M. Post. *Political Paranoia: The Psychopolitics of Hatred.* New Haven: Yale University Press, 1997.

Robinson, Jenefer. "Startle." *Journal of Philosophy* 42, no. 2 (1995): 53–74.

Rorty, Amélie Oksenberg. "User-Friendly Self-Deception." In *Self and Deception,* edited by Roger Ames and W. Dissanayake. Albany: State University of New York Press, 1996.

Rubin, Harriett. *The Princessa.* New York: Doubleday, 1997.

Sarot, Marcel. "Why Trusting God Differs from All Other Forms of Trust." *Sophia* 35, no. 1 (1996): 101–15.

Sartre, Jean-Paul. *Being and Nothingness.* Translated by Hazel Barnes. New York: Philosophical Library, 1956.

———. *The Emotions.* Translated by B. Frechtman. New York: Citadel, 1948.

Searle, John. *Intentionality.* Cambridge: Cambridge University Press, 1983.

Seligman, Adam B. *The Problem of Trust.* Princeton: Princeton University Press, 1997.

Seligman, Martin. *The Optimistic Child.* Boston: Houghton Mifflin, 1995.

Shriver, Donald W. *An Ethic for Enemies.* New York: Oxford University Press, 1995.

Singer, Irving. *The Nature of Love.* Chicago: University of Chicago Press, 1984.

Sloterdijk, Peter. *Critique of Cynical Reason.* Minneapolis: University of Minnesota Press, 1987.

Smith, Adam. *An Inquiry into the Nature and Causes of the Wealth of Nations.* New York: Hafner, 1948.

———. *The Theory of Moral Sentiments.* London: George Bell, 1880.

Solomon, Robert C. *About Love.* Lanham, Md.: Rowman and Littlefield, Madison Books, 2000.

———. *A Better Way to Think about Business.* New York: Oxford University Press, 1999.

———. *The Joy of Philosophy.* New York: Oxford University Press, 1999.

———. *A Passion for Justice.* Lanham, Md.: Rowman and Littlefield, 1994.

————. *The Passions.* Indianapolis: Hackett, 1993.

————. "Trusting." In *Festschrift for Hubert Dreyfus,* edited by J. E. Malpas and M. Wrathall. Cambridge, Mass.: MIT Press, 2000.

————. "The Virtue of Love." In *Ethical Theory: Character and Virtue,* edited by P. French, Midwest Studies in Philosophy, vol. 13. Notre Dame, Ind.: Notre Dame University Press, 1988.

Spence, Jonathan. *The Gate of Heavenly Peace.* New York: Viking, 1981.

Spinosa, Charles, Fernando Flores, and Hubert Dreyfus. *Disclosing New Worlds.* Cambridge, Mass.: MIT Press, 1997.

Tannen, Deborah. *The Argument Culture.* New York: Ballantine, 1999.

Thomas, Laurence. "Friendship." *Synthese* 72, no. 10 (1987): 217–36.

————. "Trust, Affirmation, and Moral Character: A Critique of Kantian Morality." In *Identity, Character, and Morality,* edited by Owen Flanagan and Amélie Oksenberg Rorty. Cambridge, Mass.: MIT Press, 1990.

Thucydides. *History of the Peloponnesian War.* Translated by P. Woodruff. Indianapolis: Hackett, 1993.

Tyler, Tom R. "Trust and Democratic Governance." In *Trust and Governance,* edited by Valerie Braithwaite and Margaret Levi. New York: Sage Books, 1998.

Velasquez, Manuel G. *Business Ethics.* Englewood Cliffs, N.J.: Prentice-Hall, 1982.

Webb, Mark Owen. "The Epistemology of Trust and the Politics of Suspicion." *Pacific Philosophical Quarterly* 73, no. 4 (1992): 390–99.

Whitehead, Barbara Dafoe. *The Divorce Culture.* New York: Random House/Knopf, 1996.

Whitney, John. *The Economics of Trust.* New York: McGraw-Hill, 1995.

Wicks, Andrew, Shawn Berman, and Thomas M. Jones. "The Structure of Optimal Trust: Moral and Strategic Implications." *Academy of Management Review* 24, no. 1 (1998): 99–116.

Williams, Bernard. *Ethics and the Limits of Philosophy.* Cambridge, Mass.: Harvard University Press, 1985.

————. "Formal Structures and Social Reality." In *Trust: Making and Breaking Cooperative Relations,* edited by Diego Gambetta, 3–13. New York: Blackwell, 1988.

INDEX